HEAL YOURSELF WITH CHINESE PRESSURE POINTS

Traditional Chinese Medicine practitioner
LAURENT TURLIN
WITH ALIX LEFIEF-DELCOURT

HEAL YOURSELF WITH CHINESE PRESSURE POINTS

TREAT COMMON AILMENTS AND STAY HEALTHY USING 12 KEY ACUPRESSURE POINTS

eddison
BOOKS LIMITED

This edition published in Great Britain in 2018 by
Eddison Books Limited
St Chad's House, 148 King's Cross Road,
London WC1X 9DH
www.eddisonbooks.com

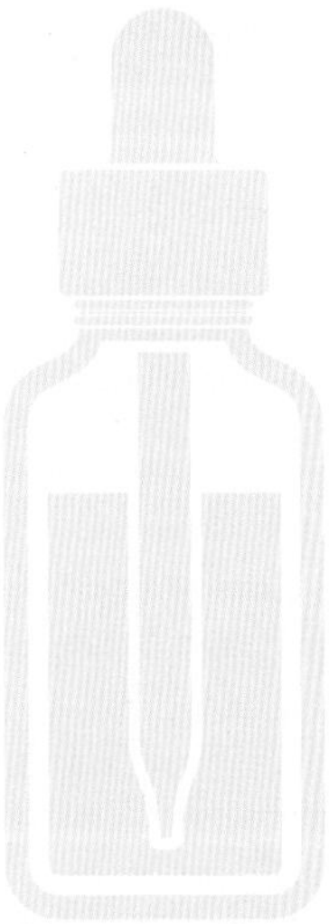

British Library Cataloguing-in-Publication
data available on request.

ISBN 978-1-85906-056-8

10 9 8 7 6 5 4 3 2 1

Printed in China

First published in France in 2017 by Leduc.s Éditions as
Automassages Chinois: Les 12 Points Essentiels

Contents

INTRODUCTION 7

1 THE PRINCIPLES OF TRADITIONAL CHINESE MEDICINE 9

2 WHAT IS ACUPRESSURE? 17

3 COMPLEMENTARY TECHNIQUES 27

4 THE 12 KEY POINTS 37

POINT No.1 **SP6** 40
POINT No.2 **St36** 42
POINT No.3 **UB40** 44
POINT No.4 **GB30** 46
POINT No.5 **CV6** 48
POINT No.6 **LI4** 50
POINT No.7 **P6** 52
POINT No.8 **Lu7** 54
POINT No.9 **TB6** 56
POINT No.10 **LI20** 58
POINT No.11 **GV26** 60
POINT No.12 **GV20** 62

5 TREATING COMMON CONDITIONS 65

Digestive Disorders 66
ENT Disorders 80
Aches & Pains 98
Gynaecological, Sexual & Urinary Disorders 126
Psychological & Nervous Disorders 138
Prevention 156

Index 157
About the Authors 160

Introduction

Acupressure is a self-massage technique integrated into Traditional Chinese Medicine. Based on the manual stimulation of energy points, or acupuncture points, it could even be described as a manual version of traditional Chinese acupuncture.

You probably never realized that Chinese acupressure already features in your daily life. When you suffer from a headache, you massage your temples to ease the pain. In the morning, when you get up, you press the inside corners of your eyes to clear your vision ... and your mind. Before starting on some work, or before a meal, you rub your hands together to stimulate your energy and your appetite.

These seemingly insignificant daily actions help stimulate all your body's major functions. This is the basic principle of acupressure – an intuitive and simple method which offers, in some cases, immediate and visible results on aches and pains, hiccups, colds, travel sickness, and more.

It also an effective remedy for many of the problems we face in our modern society. Stress, anxiety, depression, insomnia, muscular spasms and pains are all imbalances prevalent in our culture, reminding us how important it is to take care of our health. Acupressure offers a holistic solution, focusing both on prevention *and* healing at the same time.

And, finally, it is a method for the preservation of life, maintaining longevity by fighting ageing, and strengthening the body's functions and protecting it from disease. To live for as long as possible, in the best possible condition, both physically and mentally – now, isn't that a wonderful promise?

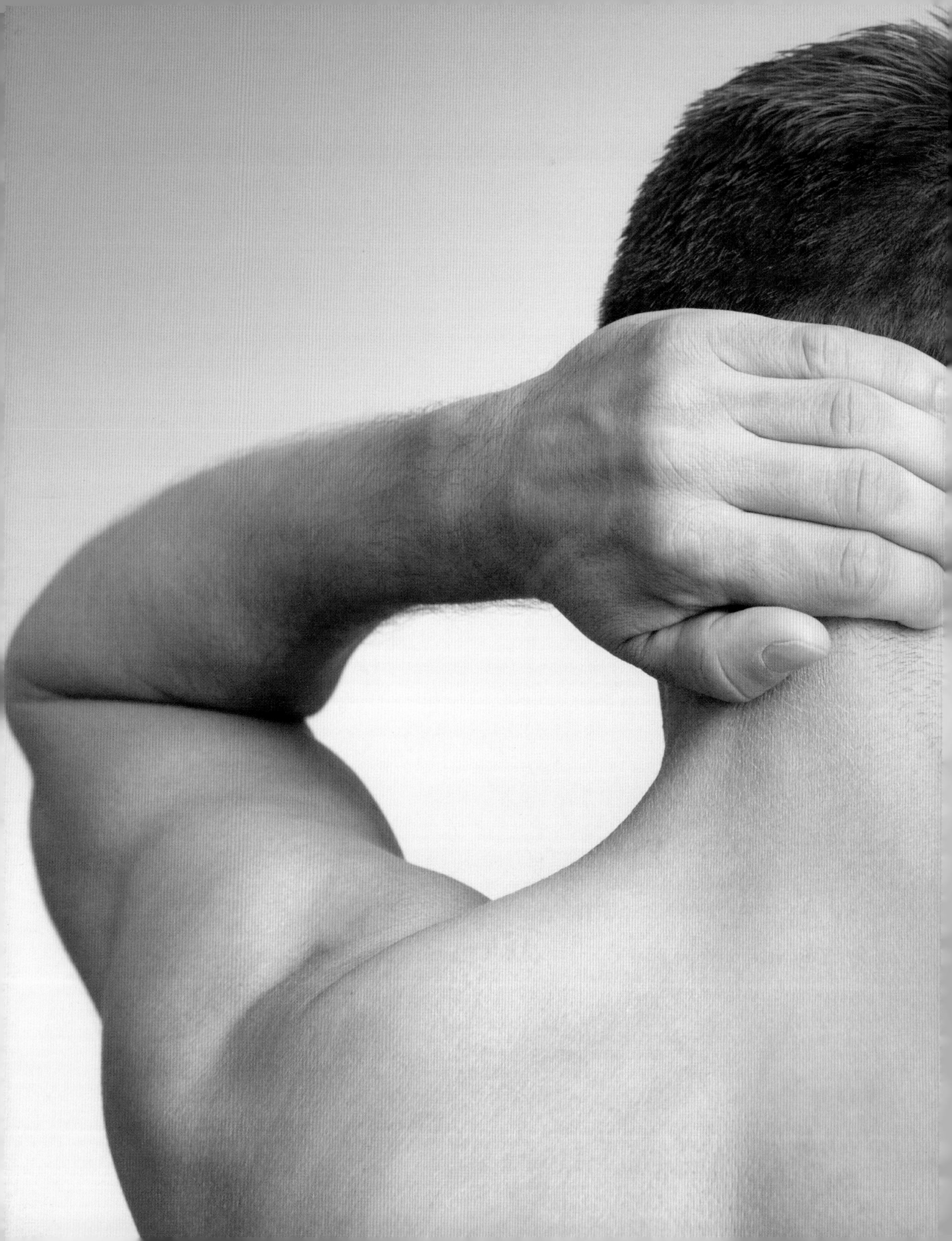

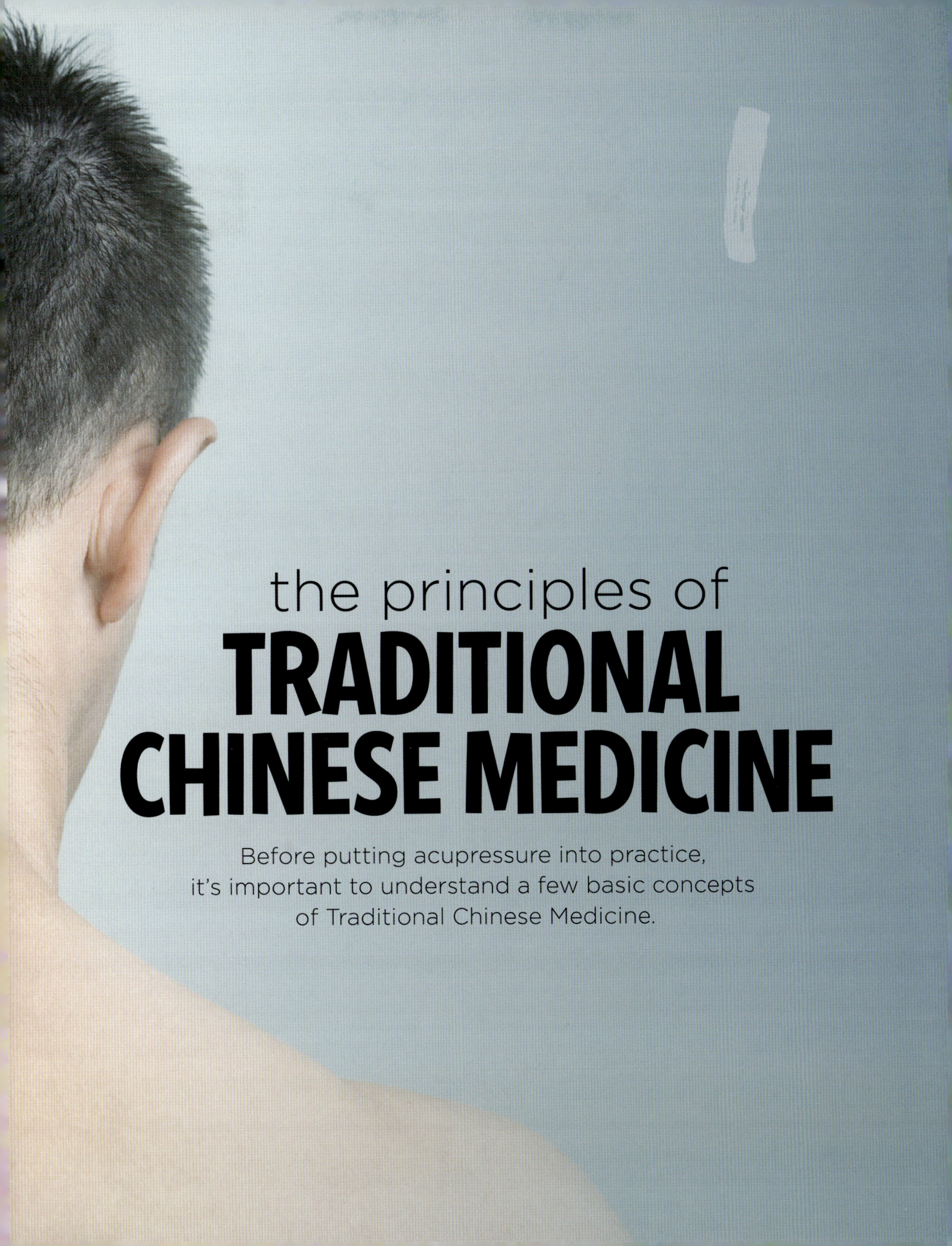

the principles of TRADITIONAL CHINESE MEDICINE

Before putting acupressure into practice, it's important to understand a few basic concepts of Traditional Chinese Medicine.

3 key concepts

QI, YIN & YANG

Traditional Chinese Medicine aims to optimize what is known as 'qi' or life force. In the Chinese tradition, qi is the source of all things: *energy is the foundation of humankind.* It's the original momentum directing all manifestations in the universe, including all living beings. It's the primordial force animating all of creation. All phenomena are produced by the movements and changes in qi. Life is a constant succession of changes in qi. Everything comes from the life force, whether on the physical, mental, emotional, intellectual, sexual or spiritual level ... The body can survive for a time without food or water, and even without breathing; but without qi – even if it's only for a second – it would face instant death. Because qi is life!

To optimize qi, we must restore the balance between yin and yang. According to Taoist thought, yin and yang are two opposing and complementary terms occurring together and alternatively. Yin and yang are the sum of two opposing aspects linked to each other: white

Yin & yang correspondences

Yang	Yin
WHITE	BLACK
MAN	WOMAN
SUN	MOON
DAY	NIGHT
UP	DOWN
OUTSIDE	INSIDE
ASCENDING	DESCENDING
MOBILE	IMMOBILE
EXCITED	INHIBITED
LIGHT	HEAVY
EXPANDING	CONTRACTING

is yang, black yin; man is yang, woman yin ... yin becoming yang and yang becoming yin endlessly, all things in relation to others entering into this universal concept.

The symbol representing yin and yang is well known. It's composed of two complementary colours: black and white. In each space, a dot in the opposite colour reminds us that the two concepts are linked, that they follow each other, and that one exists because of the other. Nothing is completely yin or completely yang. Each holds the seed of the other within itself; excess or deficiency in one has consequences on the other and creates an imbalance in the whole. It's a relationship of interdependence, where one is not conceivable without the other, and where one creates the other – for example, when day makes way for night.

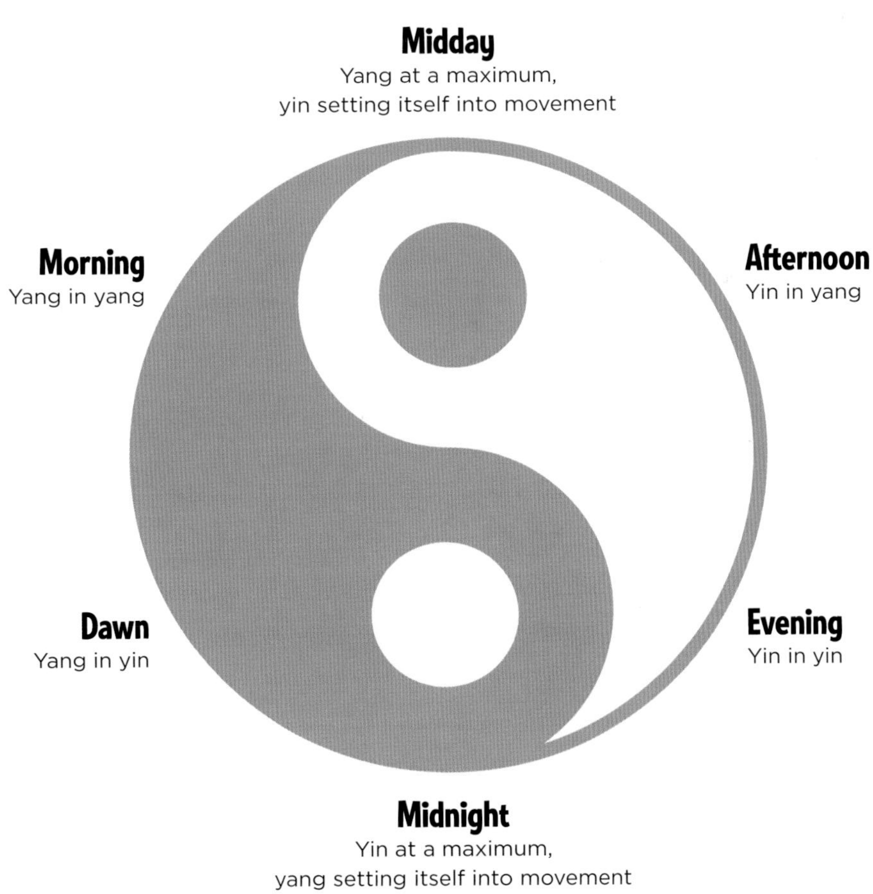

The 5 movements theory

The alternation between yin and yang takes place in a constant process of transformation. There are five energy phases, or movements (*Wu Xing*), punctuating each day. In the morning, yang rises and culminates at midday before diminishing and making way for yin, whose culminating point is midnight. The names of the five movements symbolize the nature of the dynamics they represent.

Each movement creates or produces the following movement in a defined order: the movement of wood produces/creates the movement of fire, fire creates earth, earth creates metal, which in turn creates water, which creates wood in perpetuity. In the five phases, there is also simultaneous control and inhibition. Each movement stimulates/controls another: wood controls earth, earth controls water, water controls fire, fire controls metal, and metal controls wood, until the cycle begins all over again.

This process explains the physiological relationships between the organs and bowels, between man and the world. Life is movement, and movement should be regulated and controlled. Excess or deficiency in one of the movements disturbs the overall equilibrium.

Traditional Chinese Medicine connects each of the visceral organs and each of the bowel organs to an element:

- **The liver and the gall bladder belong to wood.**
- **The heart and the small Intestine belong to fire.**
- **The spleen and the stomach belong to earth.**
- **The lungs and the large intestine belong to metal.**
- **The kidneys and the bladder belong to water.**

The main causes of disease according to Traditional Chinese Medicine

According to Traditional Chinese Medicine, disease results from an imbalance affecting one or more organs or bowels, and from an imbalance in the communication network of energy channels (the meridians). This could be due to a lack of energy, an excess of energy or a stagnation of energy. These imbalances can be linked to different causes. They may be related to climate (these are the external causes: wind, cold, humidity, heat, drought) or to emotions (these are the internal causes: anger, grief, sadness, fright, joy, worry or fear). Added to these factors are others such as stress, an unbalanced diet, an injury ...

'Disease results from an imbalance affecting one or more organs or bowels, and from an imbalance in the communication network of energy channels (the meridians).'

Among the various external causes, Traditional Chinese Medicine considers **wind as one of the main causes of disease**. It is linked to the liver, to the east, to spring, and to the wood element. It has multiple facets and corresponds to all the negative qi on which disease is based, by combining with any yin or yang imbalance. It can coexist with cold, humidity, heat or drought. As it is very mobile, wind joins other adverse elements to attack the body (external syndromes of wind-cold, wind-cold-humidity, wind-heat and wind-drought). Wind is yang. It attacks the upper part of the body (head, face, neck and skin). It can cause many symptoms: cold, headaches, and migratory pains such as rheumatism, tremors, convulsions, spasms, dizziness and instability. Wind is changeable. Like its original character in nature, it moves in different and abrupt directions with quick and unexpected fluctuations. It could, for example, lead to skin irritations with no fixed location. Internal wind is associated with a liver imbalance, with trembling, loss of balance, dizziness, contractures, spasms and convulsions.

The human body: the reunion of three treasures

Chinese tradition recognizes the fundamental nature of 'Three Treasures':

神

1 SHEN

Yang in nature, it corresponds to heaven. It descends to be incarnated in the physical heart.

精

2 JING-QI

Yin in nature, it corresponds to the earth. It is the fabric of life, incarnation. It is stored in the kidneys.

氣

3 QI

It reunites the Jing yin (earth) and the Shen yang (heaven).

QI begins from the very conception of foetal life: it is inherited from the qi of both parents' kidneys. This is the parental qi, or the qi from the 'prior heaven'. Once born, a human being consumes nutrients from the external environment to nourish its parental qi: this is the acquired source of qi, also called 'acquired qi' of the 'subsequent heaven'. This qi is produced from dietary nutrients and purified inhaled air. Parental qi and acquired qi are two different sources of the same qi.

JING OR JING-QI is the life force. This is the most subtle fabric of the matter enabling the physical body's development, regeneration, revitalization, maintenance and reproduction. It's passed down from your parents, at the time of loving conception. This is the genetic code of the family line, which passes on our specific heredity, ethnic characteristics, psycho-emotional patterns, and energetic, organic, reproductive and spiritual potential. Jing is stored in the kidneys. Like a company director (our incarnation), each individual can either make their Jing prosper or lead their company to bankruptcy (premature death) by neglecting its care.

Jing is limited and not renewable; it is the basis of longevity. It's like a wax candle: the lit candle represents fire, life's yang; the wax symbolizes Jing. The flame is the manifestation of the transformation of Jing into the energy necessary for the prosperity of life. The candle represents the length of life, conditional to the size of the candle. When we nourish ourselves with liquids, solids and air, we feed this wax, which is deposited at the base of the flame. So, the better we nourish ourselves and the better we breathe, the more this wax – and thereby our longevity – will be strengthened.

SHEN is the quintessence of qi. It is both the primordial life force and the spiritual influx. This is a fragment of the original cosmic divine spirit from heaven that we all have within us, and which descends to be incarnated in our heart at birth.

Certain signs indicate that Shen is in balance: a healthy complexion, bright, clear and expressive eyes, a calm voice and breath, coherent speech, a stable and balanced attitude. All these signs give us information on the balance of qi and the blood, the internal organs and the state of the body and the mind. In Traditional Chinese Medicine, the heart and mind are closely linked. The heart (which controls the blood, the blood vessels and mental, emotional and spiritual activities) is the seat of Shen. They form an inseparable pair: the heart is yin, an organ filled with blood and therefore tangible, while Shen is yang, intangible. The heart is the centre directing the body's perceptions. It interprets aches and pains – which are manifestations of imbalances in the qi and the blood – and reacts by raising an alarm. This also explains the link between the heart and the brain in Traditional Chinese Medicine in managing physical, psychic and mental pain. Regular self-manipulation of the key Shen points (such as point **P6**; see page 52) is also a way to optimize serenity and longevity.

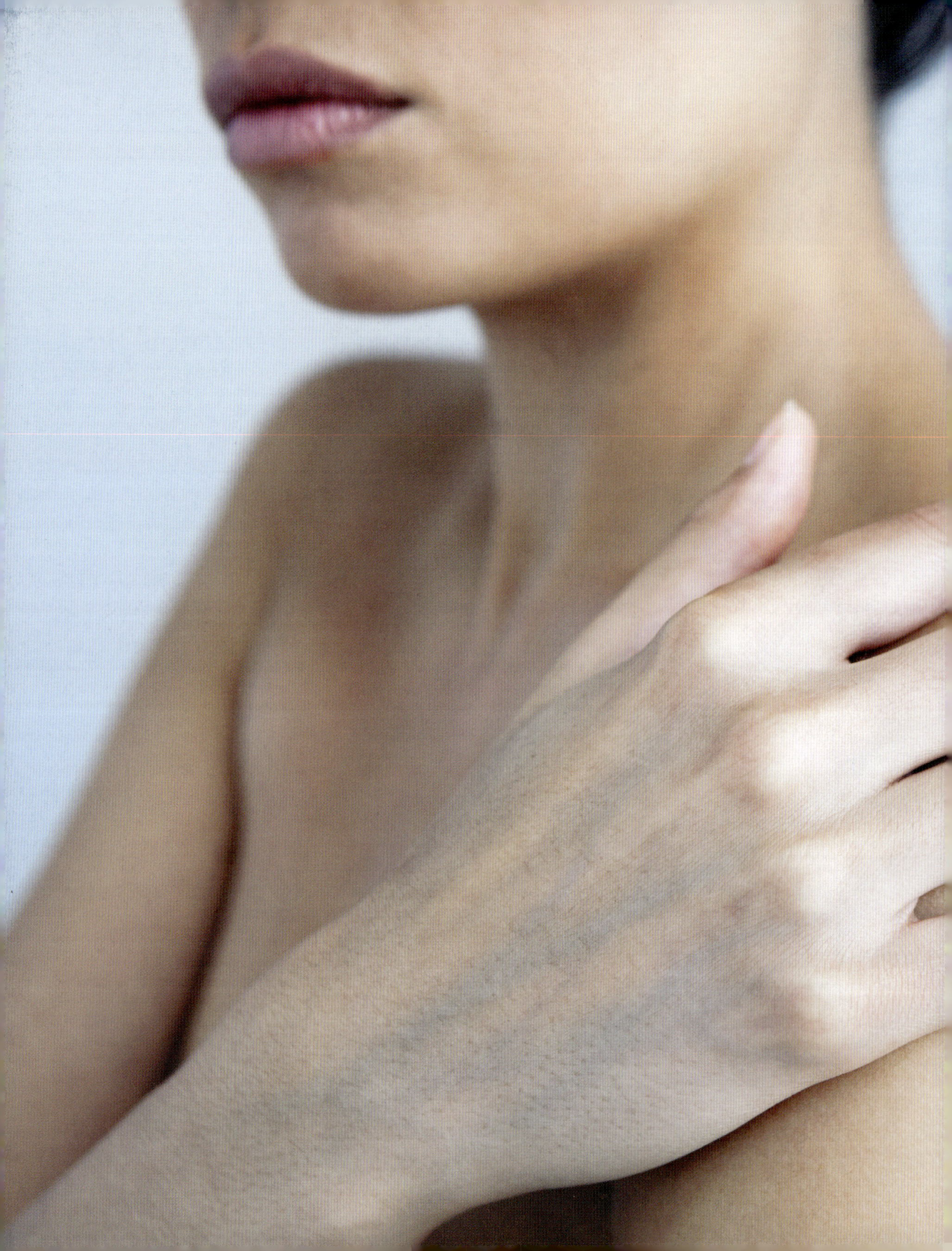

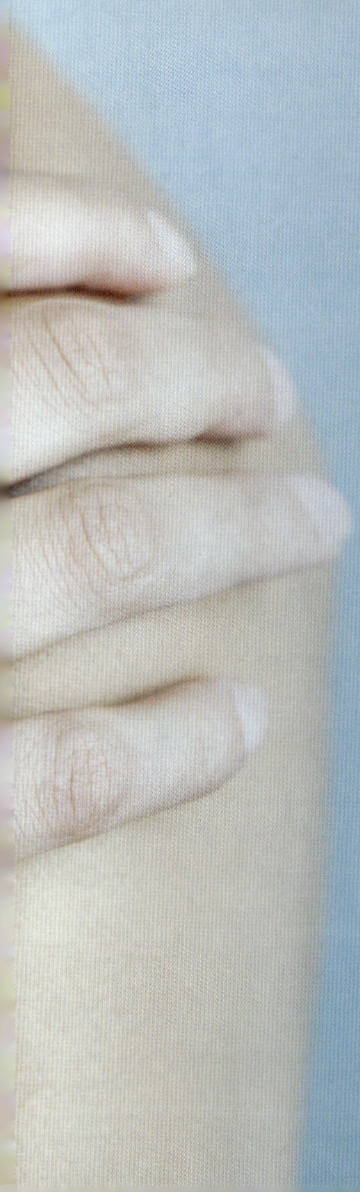

2

what is ACUPRESSURE?

Like acupuncture, acupressure aims to restore the free movement of blood, body fluids and qi between yin and yang, as well as the proper functioning of the body's overall metabolism. To achieve this, it acts on points located on energy channels within the body, known as meridians.

The system of meridians & energy points

The network of the 12 main meridians

The meridians are a network of interwoven energy pathways connecting the internal organs, and linked to the body's surface and to the environment in a broader sense. There are 12 main meridians, which form a continuous cycle in the body. The human structure is closely linked to them, and they are also connected to each other. Qi and blood flow constantly within them; they also help regulate yin, yang, the organs and the bowels. The meridians form the overall structure, setting up connections for the complex communication between all the body's parts. Through this prism, the human being, according to Chinese belief, is perceived as being inseparable from its environment. The practice of self-massage helps to harmonize this energy network on a day-to-day basis, ensuring overall balance and maintaining the foundation of life.

THE MERIDIANS CORRESPONDING TO THE Five organs:

- The main meridian of the liver (**Liv**)
- The main meridian of the lung (**Lu**)
- The main meridian of the heart (**HT**)
- The main meridian of the spleen/pancreas (**Sp**)
- The main meridian of the kidneys (**K**)

THE MERIDIANS CORRESPONDING TO THE Five bowels:

- The main meridian of the stomach (**St**)
- The main meridian of the small intestine (**SI**)
- The main meridian of the gall bladder (**GB**)
- The main meridian of the large intestine (**LI**)
- The main meridian of the bladder (**UB**)

THE MERIDIANS CORRESPONDING TO THE Two special functions:

- The main meridian of the pericardium (**P**)
- The main meridian of the Triple Burner or Triple Warmer (**TB**)
  This corresponds to the lymphatic system and thermoregulation.

A certain number of energy points are distributed over each of these meridians: there are 361 in all. In China, each point has a name personifying it (for example, *Zu San Li* for point **St36**), whereas in the West a system of letters and numbers is used, to make it easier to memorize (point **St36** is therefore the 36th point of the stomach's main meridian).

The network of 8 extraordinary vessels

In addition to this network of main meridians, there are the eight 'extraordinary' vessels, also called 'marvellous' or 'curious' meridians. Unlike the main meridians, they are not linked to the organs/bowels, and do not depend on the main directions of the regular meridians, nor do they have their own acupuncture points. They integrate the overall network of regular meridians rather like a lake, playing the role of a reservoir as they monitor the qi and the blood that overflow from the main meridians, and acting like a back-up system when the main system is deficient. Points on two of these vessels are used in this book: the Governing Vessel, and the Conception Vessel.

How to locate the points precisely

To locate the points you want to massage precisely, a special measurement system called 'cun' is used. A cun represents the length of the second phalange of the middle finger (between the tops of the two main creases, when the finger is bent). The advantage of this system is that it is based on each individual's own anatomy, and so the measurements are personalized. Varying units of this measurement can be determined using the thumb and fingers (see below), and there are also a certain number of predetermined measurements over the whole body (see overleaf).

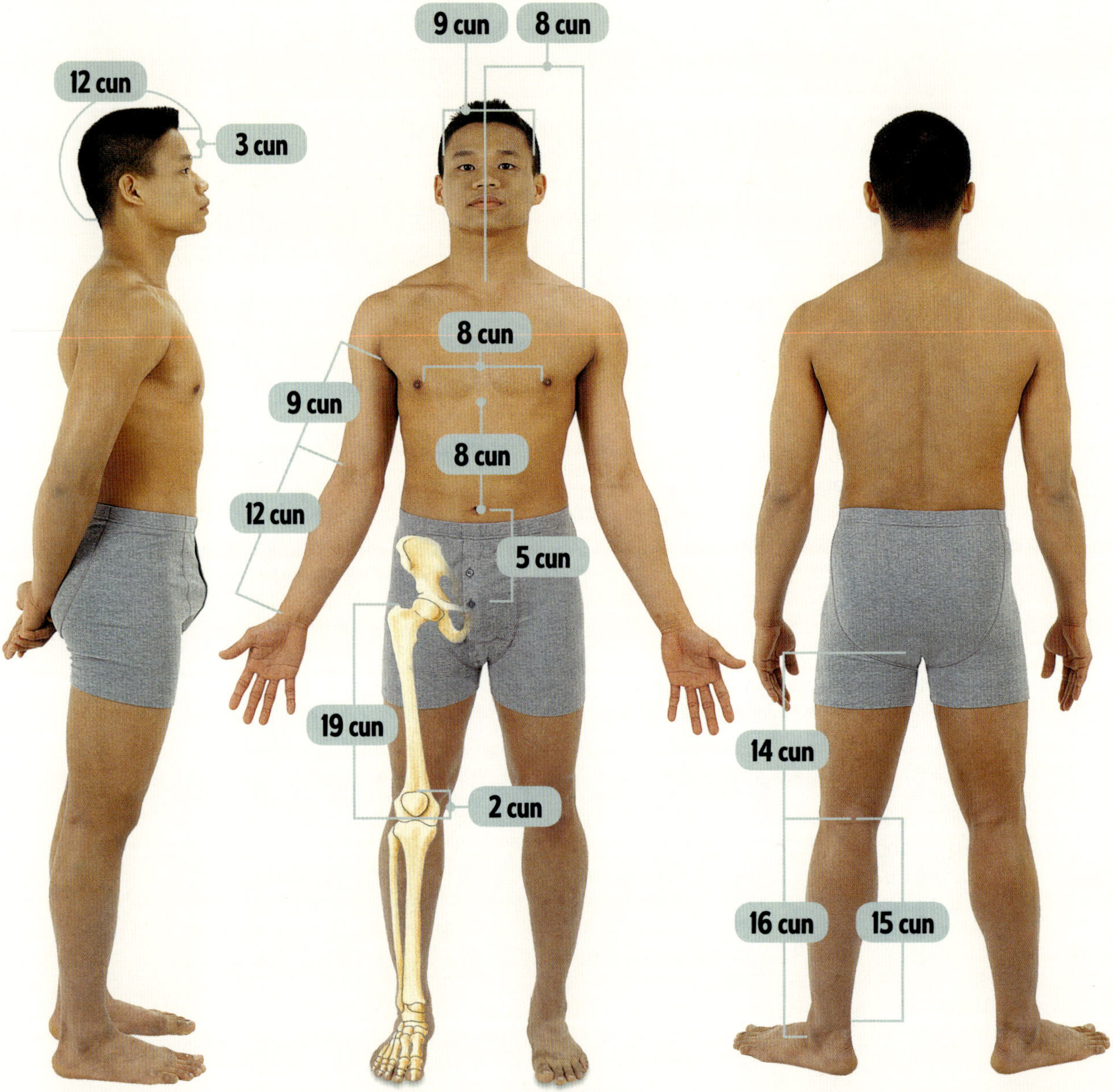
12 cun
3 cun
9 cun
8 cun
8 cun
9 cun
8 cun
12 cun
5 cun
19 cun
2 cun
14 cun
16 cun
15 cun

What is acupressure used for?

Acupressure has many benefits. The technique can help us to:

- **clear physical and emotional blocks,** the source of aches and pains or alleviate disease. In practical terms, it acts on digestion, elimination, breathing, and physical and sexual tone.
- **improve our health** by stimulating the immune system. Acupressure therefore has a preventative effect.
- **develop flexibility.** Self-massage also has an effect on ligaments and joints. By strengthening these, it increases physical strength and resistance, as well as helping to develop resistance to disease.
- **increase longevity.** Acupressure is a preventative practice used to extend life. Certain points (like **P6**) are particularly significant from this perspective.
- **rediscover peace and serenity.** On a psychological level, it helps boost our self-esteem and self-confidence, our self-regard, and our joie de vivre and motivation. It is also very effective when preparing for exams, before a job interview, a first date, before a meeting or a presentation in front of an audience ... essentially before any important event that could bring on stage fright or stress and requires some form of action to calm us down.

Whatever our initial indication or symptom may be, acupressure's ultimate aim is to help each one of us to be centred, to rediscover our inner peace, and to protect ourselves from the aggressions of the outside world while remaining strong and calm - in short, to acquire good health, a strengthened physique, and a calm and efficient mind.

How acupressure works on pain

In Traditional Chinese Medicine, the main cause of pain is the stagnation of qi and blood. This could possibly be due to a poor diet, physical trauma, an inherited weakness of qi, stress, an unhealthy lifestyle ... not forgetting emotional factors such as an excess of joy, fear, anxiety, anger, grief, and so on. External factors also play a role: wind, cold, heat, humidity and dryness.

This blockage of qi prevents the proper nourishment of the cells, tissues, muscles, organs and glands. Under normal circumstances, the body easily restores itself back to health and vitality. But if the disturbance in qi is prolonged or excessive, or the body is weakened, the movement of qi no longer takes place correctly. Various symptoms - especially pain - may then begin to manifest. Here, pain is a natural alarm signal expressing a blockage.

It's important for qi to move freely inside the whole body. Imagine water flowing through a hosepipe: if the hose is blocked, it won't supply an adequate quantity of water to the plant, and the plant won't be able to grow and bloom. Acupuncture and acupressure are an alternative to the classic methods of pain treatment because they treat the root of the problem, without any side effects. When the original cause of the pain is corrected, your body can begin to heal at a deeper level. The World Health Organization has recognized the benefits of acupuncture in the treatment and elimination of pain in a large number of pathologies (including neck pain, sciatica, sprains, tennis elbow, headaches and lower back pain).

Who is acupressure for?

Acupressure is suitable for all: children as well as adults, the young as well as the old, hyperactive people who seek serenity and calm, as well as those who are tired and want to boost their energy.

However, caution must be taken in certain cases:

- **Babies and children:** since their energetic bodies are different (as they are still in the growing phase), acupressure is practised mainly on the hands and face.
- **Older people:** moxibustion is more commonly used. This technique, based on stimulating the key points with heat, helps to effectively tone the overall body (see page 32).
- **During pregnancy,** acupressure can be very useful in combating a number of specific minor ailments (such as nausea, for example). But caution must be exercised, as certain points are strictly prohibited during this period. Among the 12 points covered in this book, some are prohibited throughout pregnancy. This applies to points **LI4** and **Sp6**. In addition, **CV6** is prohibited from the start of the third month. Furthermore, never stimulate any points located below the abdomen or the sacrolumbar (lower back) area. Touch and pressure must also be applied more gently on the lymphatic areas: throat, groin, ears and outer chest (near the armpits). Always remain attentive to your body.
- **People who are ill and/or receiving medical treatment** are encouraged to consult their doctor before practising these self-massage techniques. If you suffer from certain serious diseases (intestinal cancer, tuberculosis, heart disease, leukaemia, epilepsy, or serious neurological and nerve disorders), avoid practising acupressure on the abdominal area. This also applies if you wear a pacemaker.

Also bear in mind the following few contraindications when practising acupressure:

- If you are suffering from a **serious burn,** do not apply pressure directly on the affected area until it has completely healed.
- Never practise acupressure **on a recently formed scar** or on a tumour.
- **After an injury or a surgical operation,** do not apply direct pressure on the affected area for a month. After this period, gradually apply pressure with your finger to allow the layers of tissue to respond in a therapeutic way. If an area is very sensitive when you apply pressure, apply it more gently.
- Do not practise acupressure on yourself on or others **if you are angry or under the influence of alcohol or drugs.**

Is belief necessary for it to work?

Absolutely not! There's proof that the method works even on animals; if your cat or dog is suffering from pain on a particular point, he will let you massage this painful area. However, something else we can be sure of is this: if we put our intention and determination into the technique, with a positive outlook, the method works even faster. Action with intention boosts the result!

PLEASE NOTE!
In some cases, acupressure may turn out to be too painful, or may induce nausea or headaches. In these instances, it's important to always remain attentive to your body, so that you can adjust and adapt the pressure accordingly.

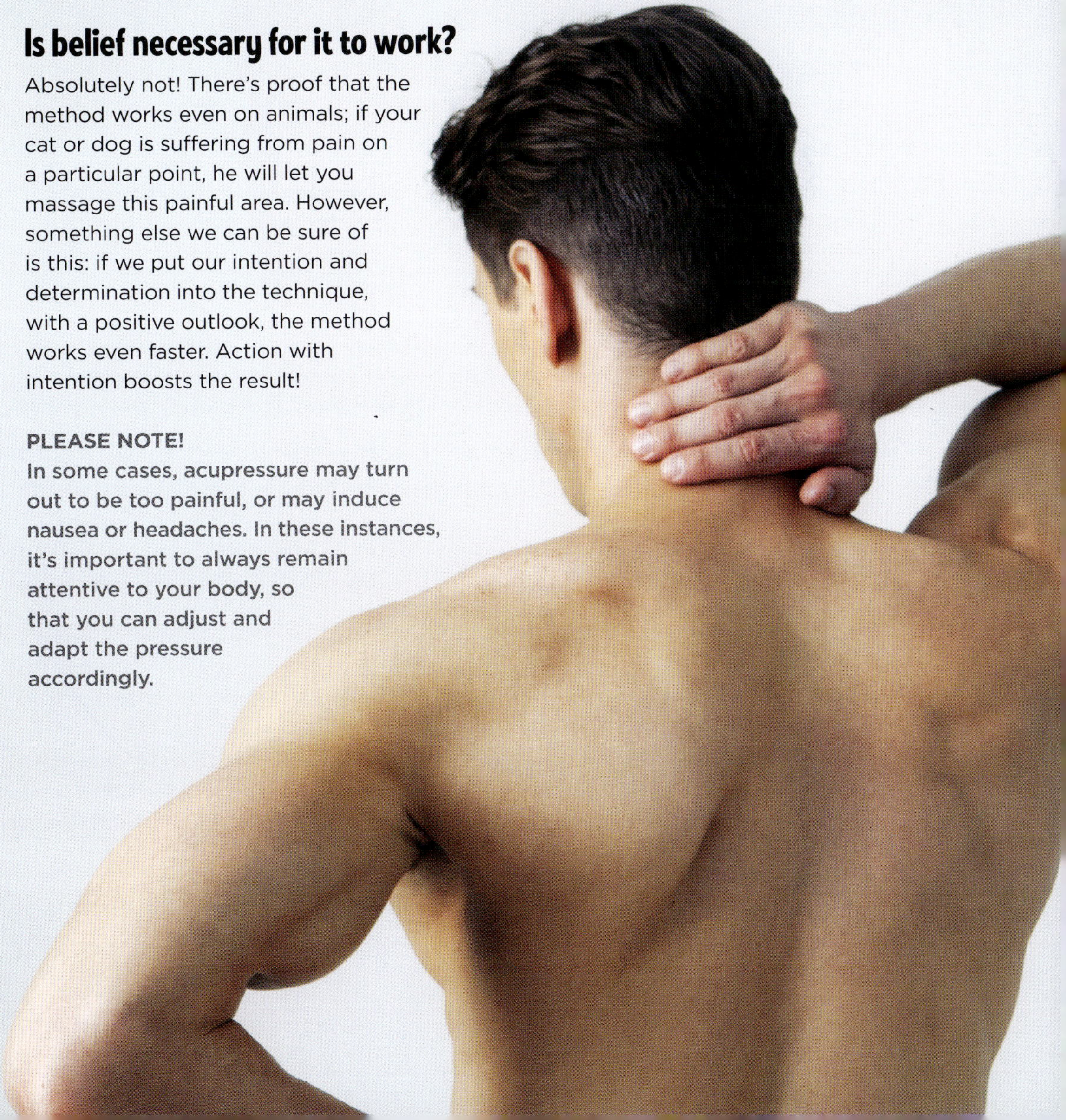

How do you perform a good self-massage?

The good news is that no particular equipment is required. You can apply pressure on the different points using your thumb, fingertip or your knuckle. You can also use a massage stick (a kind of small chopstick made of wood or crystal), or even just a pencil or pen.

There are three main ways to massage the points:

1 Dispersion The massage is done in an anti-clockwise direction, by applying a little strength. The aim is to remove the energy blockage causing the pain or symptoms.

2 Tonification The massage is done in a clockwise direction, gently, usually with the thumb. This helps treat states of deficiency.

3 Harmonization The massage can be done in any direction, using medium pressure (neither too strong nor too gentle). Unlike the two preceding methods, this massage is carried out without any particular intention. When you're not sure which method to use, this is the ideal one.

Acupressure is not about massaging precise points in a rush, or while you're doing something else. To be effective, you need to prepare yourself and adopt some good habits ...

RELAX

Take a break from your daily life. Find a calm and airy place. Switch off your mobile phone and stay away from screens (computer, tablet, TV ...). Light a candle, burn some incense, or spray a relaxing essential oil (English lavender essential oil works well). Play some relaxing music.

VISUALIZE

Visualization allows you to put intention into the action, since energy follows thought. Visualize your own body, the movements you make, the points you are going to massage ... While you are manipulating the point, visualize a turquoise radius (a colour which has a healing action) around the point. As you massage, imagine, for example, that you're draining away the colour black, and that the area is transforming into golden light.

MEDITATE

Brief and very simple meditation exercises have a beneficial effect on Shen. They help you achieve a calm and serene state before a self-massage session. For example: sit comfortably on a chair, feet touching the floor, close your eyes, relax your shoulders, breathe quietly and visualize a gold thread at the top of your head. Feel your feet anchored to the floor and imagine that a golden light is entering your head and spreading inside your whole body, by sending the physical, emotional and organic impurities into the ground to be transformed there. With each breath, the golden light of heaven flows down to your feet in a cycle of self-regeneration. You could also do this exercise standing up, like an internal Qi Gong practice. Remember that energy follows thought; where your thoughts go, your energy goes too. The brain does not distinguish between reality and virtual reality.

BREATHE

Breathing is an important factor. It helps harmonize energy, regulates the heart (central to our emotions) and has an effect on the nervous system. The notion of cardiac coherence is essential: there's a close connection between the heart and the brain. When we are faced with a stressful situation, emotions surface and have repercussions on the heart, which beats more rapidly. Conversely, by breathing calmly, and therefore controlling your heart rate, you can influence the brain and the nervous system. The aim of cardiac coherence is therefore to learn how to control your breath in order to stay calm. To practise: spend five minutes taking long and deep inhalations by expanding your belly, then contract it as you blow out the air.

3

complementary TECHNIQUES

- Essential oils
- Moxibustion

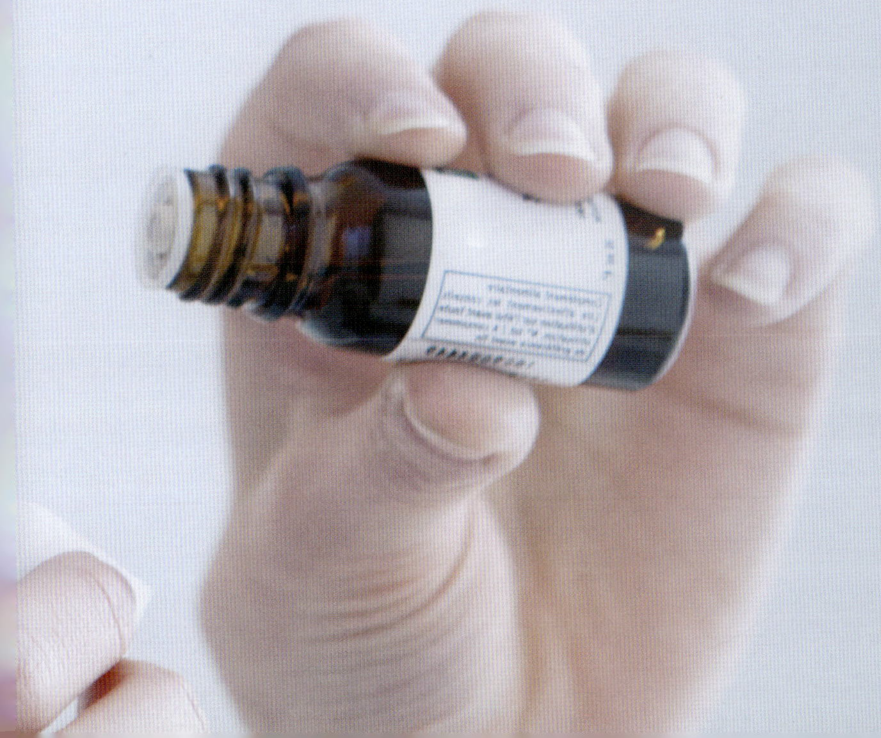

Essential oils

Essential oils are volatile substances extracted from certain aromatic plants (leaves, flowers, zest, wood, bark, grains, pine needles ...). They come in liquid form and are very fragrant. Each essential oil has a chemical composition. In ancient cultures - especially in China - more than 2,000 years ago, essences and aromatic plants were commonly used for therapeutic reasons (to combat epidemics, for example, plants such as cinnamon, pepper, ginger, and so on, would be used). Essential oils are are still widely used in Traditional Chinese Medicine today.

Essential oils can be used in different ways:

INTERNALLY - in other words, by ingesting them. There are several techniques for this: you can either deposit drops of essential oil directly under the tongue (in certain specific cases) or drop them on a neutral tablet or a sugar cube and let it dissolve in your mouth, or, alternatively, you can mix them into a little honey or plant oil.

PLEASE NOTE: Always follow directions for use carefully, as not all essential oils can be ingested.

EXTERNALLY - for massage, inhalation or diffused into the air. To use on the skin, first mix the essential oil into a carrier plant oil (such as sweet almond, olive, grape seed). In some specific cases, and for certain essential oils only, you can also apply them undiluted. In this way, the essences can penetrate gently into the body through the pores and are delivered to the appropriate organ or targeted area via the blood, often referred to as 'tropism', and detailed throughout this book as 'corresponding areas' (see opposite). Due to their active molecular structures, essential oils act on the physical, mental, emotional and spiritual body. Applying the essential oil on acupressure points helps you boost the intended action of stimulation.

'Due to their active molecular structures, essential oils act on the physical, mental, emotional and spiritual body.'

Examples of essential oils and corresponding areas

- Lungs: eucalyptus globulus essential oil, niaouli essential oil
- Spleen/pancreas: geranium rosat essential oil
- Gall bladder: peppermint essential oil, rosemary essential oil
- Prostate: sandalwood essential oil
- Bladder: juniper essential oil, oregano essential oil

PLEASE NOTE!
Once extracted, an essential oil can be kept on average for two to five years, away from light and heat in a tinted glass bottle. Be careful to always close the bottle immediately after use to prevent oxidation, which is a major factor in the product's deterioration.

Another way to use essential oils is by diffusion. For example, it can help you sanitize and purify a room, or create an environment conducive to sleep. Essential oils can also be used for direct inhalation, after an emotional shock, to improve concentration, get rid of a migraine, or, quite simply, to help you feel better.

Different essential oils are used in the following pages of this book. Here are the main ones, with their properties.

Eucalyptus radiata [black peppermint] essential oil (*Eucalyptus radiata*) is principally used to treat the upper respiratory tract. It acts on the nasopharyngeal area and combats virus outbreaks. With its subtle and airy smell, it's the most pleasant to inhale of all the eucalyptus essential oils, and is less overpowering than eucalyptus globulus essential oil. Its very effective in combating winter illnesses such as bronchitis, colds, flu, nasopharyngitis and sinusitis.

How is it used? Apply it on the skin (diluted in a little plant oil) or use for steam inhalation (1 drop in a bowl of hot water), or via diffusion in the air (always together with another non-irritant essential oil for the mucous membranes).

Caution! Not to be used on children under the age of 6 years and on pregnant women. Always use it diluted in a little plant oil, as it can be an irritant for the mucous membranes.

Ginger essential oil (*Zingiber officinalis*) is especially recommended for treating mild digestive disorders (such as nausea, vomiting, travel sickness) and combating fatigue.

How is it used? Apply it on the skin (diluted in a little plant oil) or use via inhalation or diffusion.

Caution! Never use it undiluted. It is prohibited during the first three months of pregnancy, while breast-feeding, and for children under the age of 3 years.

Rosemary cineole essential oil (*Rosmarinus officinalis L. cineoliferum*) is recommended for all respiratory infections. It can be used both for prevention and treatment.

How is it used? By diffusion in the surrounding air as a disinfectant, or by applying it on the skin (diluted in plant oil).

Tea tree essential oil (*Melaleuca alternifolia*) is a bactericide renowned for its antibacterial, antiviral and antifungal proper properties, and can destroy all types of germs.

How is it used? By applying it on the skin (diluted in a little plant oil). It can also be diffused to sanitize the surrounding air, together with an essential oil with a more gentle smell (it is quite pungent!).

Cypress essential oil (*Cupressus sempervirens*) is mainly used for its effect on the blood circulation. It also has decongestant properties and can aid the respiratory system.

How is it used? Apply it on the skin (diluted in a little plant oil).

Caution! It is prohibited for pregnant and breast-feeding women, and in cases of cancer pathologies.

Black spruce essential oil

(*Picea mariana*) has natural hormonal properties. It is ideal for recharging the kidneys and the body – for example, during convalescence.

How is it used? It can be used undiluted for massaging into the solar plexus or the adrenals.

Caution! It can be dermocaustic (a skin irritant). Do not use in early pregnancy or on children.

Peppermint essential oil

(*Mentha piperita*) is principally recommended for its anaesthetizing properties (bumps and knocks, migraine, sciatica, tendinitis), digestive properties (indigestion, nausea, vomiting) and stimulating properties (fatigue). It is also effective for relieving minor skin conditions (such as eczema and nettle rash) and ENT infections.

How is it used? Apply it locally, on a small area. It can also be taken internally (1 drop under the tongue in the case of nausea, for example).

Caution! Not to be used on children under the age of 8 years or on pregnant and breast-feeding women. Do no apply too close to the eyes, as it can cause irritation.

Spikenard essential oil

(*Nardostachys jatamansi*) has very interesting calming properties, particularly in the case of strong emotions. It can also be used for its venotonic properties (improving circulation in the veins), in the case of varicose veins and haemorrhoids.

How is it used? Apply it locally on the solar plexus.

Niaouli essential oil

(*Melaleuca quinquenervia*) is used in cases of winter viral infections. It has anti-infectious expectorant properties. It is also a good decongestant for the veins (varicose veins, haemorrhoids).

How is it used? Apply it on the skin (diluted in a little plant oil), or use via inhalation or diffusion.

Caution! Never use it undiluted. It is prohibited during the first three months of pregnancy, while breast-feeding, and for children under the age of 3 years.

CAUTION!

Essential oils must be handled with great care. They are particularly effective when used correctly and wisely, but also present many contraindications (the price you have to pay, so to speak!).

- Always follow the dosage and directions given in this book. Do not improvise! Some essential oils can be toxic, especially if used internally over a long period of time and with high doses, such as clary sage, thuja or marjoram essential oil, which can bring on convulsions. Others, which can cause miscarriage, are prohibited for pregnant women.
- Before use, it's always a good idea to test the oil on a part of your skin (such as the elbow crease) to make sure your skin isn't allergic to it.
- If you have a skin reaction, or some essential oil gets in your eyes, rinse with a plant oil. If you have accidentally ingested an essential oil that should not be taken internally, immediately swallow 1 tablespoon of plant oil (olive oil, for example) and contact the nearest poison control centre.

Moxibustion

Moxibustion is a widely used method in Traditional Chinese Medicine (as well as in Japanese, Tibetan, Korean and Mongolian traditional medicine). It consists of stimulating certain acupuncture points with heat in order to rebalance the energies. To diffuse this heat, sticks or cones called 'moxas' are used, the ends of which are burned with a flame. These moxas are made from dried mugwort leaves, reduced to small pieces or a powder, then compressed into rolls or cones.

The practice of moxibustion involves burning the end of the stick, then holding this smouldering end a few centimetres (an inch or so) from the skin, over a specific acupuncture point, to rebalance the energies. The objective is to warm up and encourage the movement of energy and blood; according to Chinese medicine, pain is, in fact, caused by an obstruction of blood and energy (see page 21). Moxibustion also fortifies the kidneys and the overall yang in the body, eliminates wind, revitalizes the blood and dissolves stasis.

MUGWORT

Mugwort (*Artemisia vulgaris* or *Artemisia argyi*) is a herbaceous plant commonly found in temperate regions, growing freely along the roadside and on wasteland. Also known by other names, including 'St John's Plant' (not to be confused with St John's Wort), it has been renowned for its medicinal properties since antiquity. One of the herbs used in Chinese pharmacology, the Chinese sometimes refer to it as the 'plant of doctors'.

The 5 effects of moxibustion

1 **Warms the meridians**
2 **Directs the free movement of energy and blood**
3 **Strengthens yang energy and remedies breakdown/collapse**
4 **Prevents disease and maintains the lifeblood**
5 **Strengthens and regulates immunity**

Various indications of moxibustion

Moxibustion is used to:

- **relieve rheumatism and other joint problems**, due to both the bitter and pungent properties of the mugwort leaves. The pungent property is revitalizing, and energizes the qi, while the bitterness promotes the elimination of heaviness in the joints.
- **clear the respiratory system**, especially in cases of asthma, bronchitis, and so on.
- **stimulate the digestive system** – for example, in cases of abdominal pains, diarrhoea, constipation.
- **boost the circulation system**, in cases of bad circulation, hypertension, and so on.
- **treat menstrual disorders** (for example, irregular periods, heavy periods) **and those of libido** (such as impotency, frigidity).
- **fight microbial infections and tumours**. Doctors of Traditional Chinese Medicine often use it for this property; moxibustion does, in fact, promote the increase in the number of white corpuscles, which play an essential role in the body's ability to defend itself from microbial attacks.
- **strengthen immune defences and vitality**. Moxibustion stimulates the production of T lymphocytes – white corpuscles which play a central role in cellular immunity. By applying moxibustion on the acupuncture points, we can regulate the body's functions and support the body by stimulating our immune defences. Here, moxibustion is prophylactic: it is used for prevention, as an optimum way to maintain good health. Even today, in China, preventative moxibustion is practised according to age and region. The more cold, windy and humid the climate, the more moxibustion will be applied (point **St36**, for example, is traditionally used to prevent flu-like symptoms and attacks from cold and humidity; see also page 156).
- **combat fatigue.**
- **maintain glowing skin.**
- **strengthen energy and joie de vivre.**
- **boost the hair's shine and volume.**

What happens during a moxibustion session

Here's what you need to do:

1 **Prepare your equipment.** You will need a moxa stick, an ashtray or a small bowl (to collect the ashes), a lit candle and a teaspoon.

2 **Find a very stable space** (a table, for example). Never practise moxibustion directly on the floor or on a bed, to prevent any accidents with the candle.

3 **Place the end of the moxa stick on the lit candle.** Wait until the flame ignites the end of the stick and then blow on it, as if fanning the flames of a barbecue. The end of the moxa stick should be glowing and burning slowly and steadily. Be careful: it can heat up to 670°C (1238°F)!

4 **Hold the moxa stick a few centimetres (an inch or so) from the skin** near the specified points, according to the selected technique (see below).

5 Using the handle of a spoon, **tap the end of the glowing moxa stick regularly above the ashtray or bowl.** It's essential to do this, to prevent the ash from falling on the skin and causing a burn.

6 **Blow regularly on the end of the moxa stick** to kindle the glowing red tip. This ensures that the heat is maintained for the entire session. Stop the moxibustion when the skin becomes red and the sensation of heat is stable over the area.

7 At the end of the session, **don't forget to extinguish the moxa stick.** The best way to do this is to put the flame out in some soil (in a flowerpot, for example) or put it into a cigar tube to deprive it of oxygen, which will extinguish it completely. It's worth noting that holding it under water isn't always enough to put the stick out completely, especially if you only do it quickly, as the combustion could continue to spread, slowly but surely. After the stick is used and extinguished, you can reuse it for another session (a stick may be used for four or five sessions, on average). Simply take care to remove the ash deposits with a handkerchief, paper tissue or cotton wool, to clean the end as much as possible.

Two ways to apply moxa

Mild-warm method: hold the moxa stick perpendicularly over the point, about 3 cm (just over 1 in) from the skin, for 5 to 10 minutes (until the area becomes red). Regularly move it away from the skin and back again during the entire session. The sensation of heat should be bearable.

Sparrow-pecking method: without burning the skin, drop the end of the lit stick repeatedly on the point, like a sparrow pecking for seeds. Move the stick from left to right or in a circular motion, close to the area to be heated.

Precautions

Due to the strong heat emitted from moxa sticks, some precautions must be taken:

- Never apply the moxa sticks **on a body showing signs of heat:** fever (more than 38°C/100.4°F), excessive perspiration, loss of blood, generalized oedema. Moxibustion is also prohibited when the skin is red or the area is hot or burned.
- **During menopause,** it's preferable to consult a doctor or certified practitioner regarding the application of the technique. In certain very specific cases, moxibustion can be applied but not as self-treatment; without sufficient knowledge of the energy principles, it could aggravate the signs of heat and bring about a greater imbalance.
- Do not practise moxibustion **if you have just eaten.** Wait at least two hours!
- **For pregnant women,** moxibustion practice is prohibited on the lower abdomen, abdomen, sacroiliac joints and the lumbar vertebrae.
- Do not practise moxibustion **on anyone who is undernourished or has a very weak constitution.**
- Exercise caution with **people who are diabetic,** as their skin can get easily infected.
- Never carry out moxibustion sessions **on varicose veins, venous ulcers or arteritis** and, in general, **on people with poor blood circulation.** In such cases, consult a doctor or certified practitioner of traditional Chinese therapies.
- Never practise moxibustion **on anyone who is intoxicated or angry.**
- **Avoid practising moxibustion on your face,** as it could cause suppuration and leave scars.
- Moxibustion must not be practised **on certain acupuncture points** (these will be specified throughout the book).

4

the 12 KEY POINTS

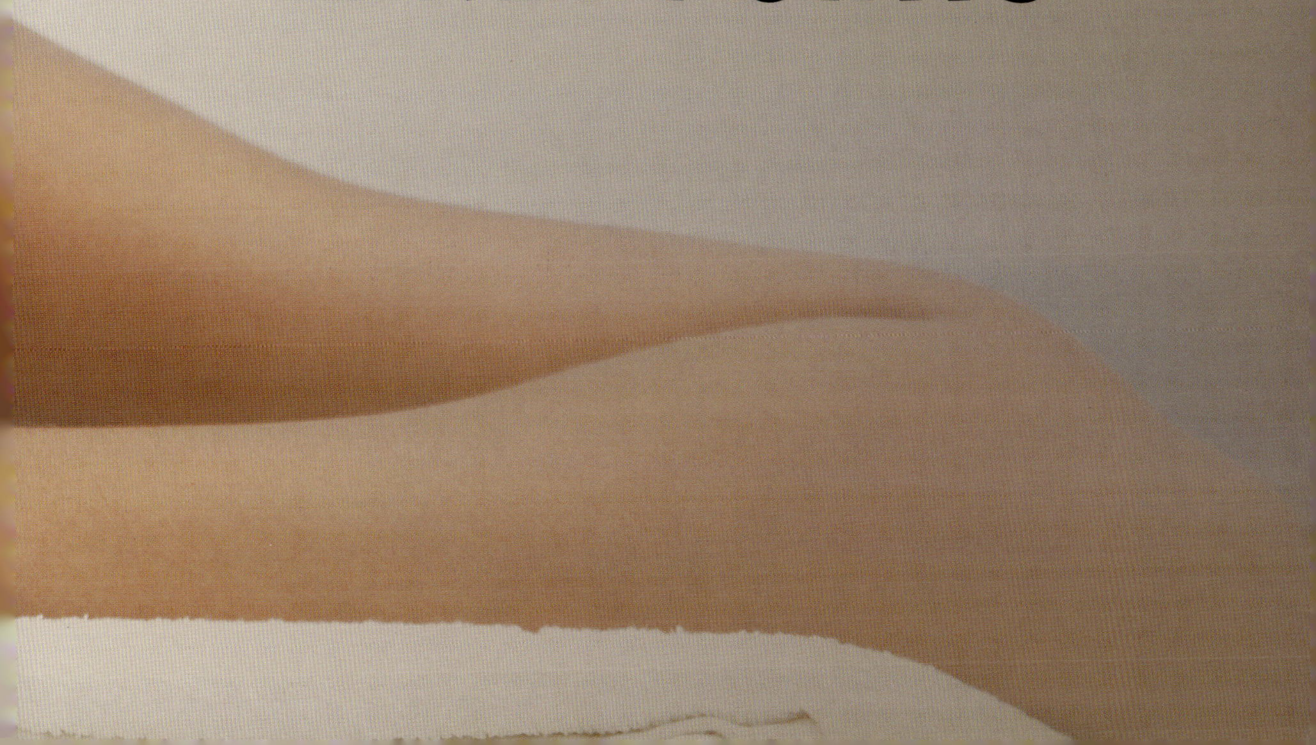

The 12 points & their spheres of action

The 12 acupuncture points presented in this book have been carefully chosen after studying several classic texts of Chinese medicine: the *Zhen Jiu Ju Ying* ('The flowers of acupuncture and moxibustion'), and the *Zhen Jiu Da Cheng* ('The great success of acupuncture and moxibustion'), as well as a key article published in July/August 1996 in the *Zhen Jiu Lin Chuang Za Zhi* (Review of the Acupuncture-Moxibustion Clinic). These texts give symptomatic indications on the four general points (**Lu7**, **LI4**, **UB40** and **St36**) which are included in this book, as well as the points that are most often used in clinical practice.

The advantage is that we don't need to differentiate between the symptoms in order to use these points. They are highly practical, as they can be used in situations of deficiency, abundance, emergency, cold or heat, chronic conditions or acute pain.

These 12 points act on certain parts of the body. They have specific effects on the areas with which they have a relationship, referred to as tropism (corresponding areas). These points scan, so to speak, the human anatomical geography. They give us a broad - and practical - method for relieving aches and pains. This system is also easy to remember, as a limited number of points are used (as opposed to the hundreds of different acupuncture points that exist).

GV20	head	**Lu7**	head, nape of neck
LI20	nose	**LI4**	face, mouth, nose
GV26	emergency cases	**GB30**	thighs, legs
CV6	immune system	**UB40**	back, lumbar region
TB6	sides/flanks	**St36**	abdomen, stomach
P6	heart, chest	**Sp6**	lower abdomen

PLEASE NOTE! Apart from GV20, GV26 and CV6, all points shown here are found on both sides of the body.

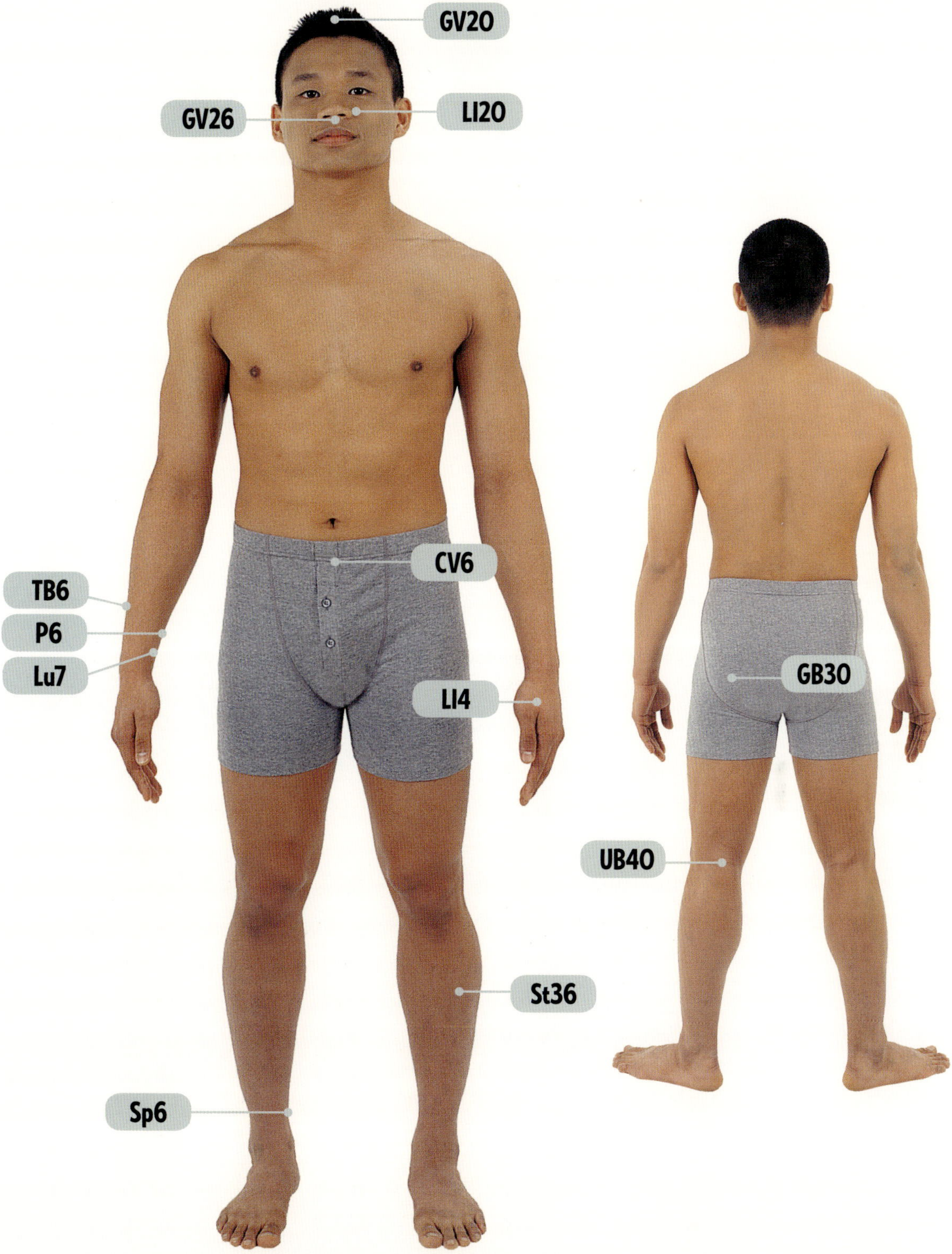
GV20
GV26
LI20
CV6
TB6
P6
Lu7
LI4
St36
Sp6
GB30
UB40

POINT No.1

SP6

San Yin Jiao

THREE YIN INTERSECTION

Regulator of the lower abdomen

LOCATION

On the inner surface of the leg, 3 cm (1⅕ in) from the top of the malleolus (bony protuberance on the ankle), at the back of the internal part of the tibia, in the depression at the edge of the bone. This point is often sensitive to pressure.

CAUTION!

Stimulation of this point is strictly prohibited if you are pregnant, due to the risk of triggering uterine contractions and miscarriage.

PRESSURE POINT SP6: OVERVIEW

CORRESPONDING AREA

Hypogastria (lower stomach/gynaecological area)

ENERGY FUNCTIONS

- Invigorates the spleen and the stomach
- Harmonizes the liver and strengthens the kidneys
- Eliminates impure elements and humidity through diuresis
- Invigorates the blood
- Treats pelvic disorders
- Supports the spleen's function of transportation and transformation
- Nourishes the blood and yin, regulates menstruation and induces labour
- Regulates urination, has beneficial effects on the genital organs and harmonizes the Lower Burner (the lower section of the Triple Burner)
- Calms the mind (Shen)

INDICATIONS

- Gynaecological and obstetric disorders
- Sterility, delayed labour, premenstrual tension
- Sexual dysfunction for men
- Impotence, involuntary ejaculation
- Difficulties with urination, urinary incontinence
- Diarrhoea, heaviness in the limbs, oedema
- Palpitations, insomnia, arterial hypertension
- Leg pain, painful blockage of the lower limbs
- Skin rash, eczema

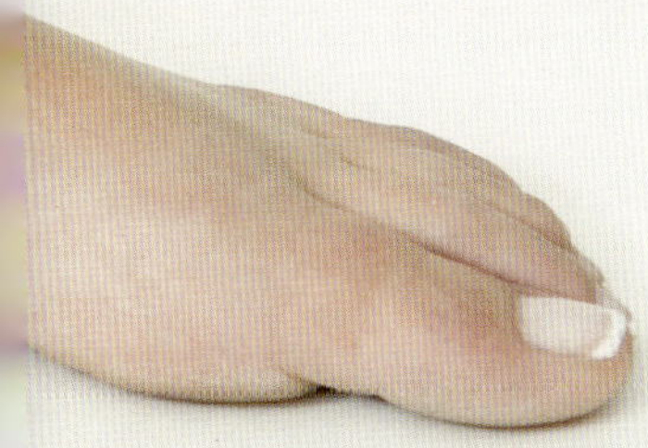

AN EXTRA TIP

This point is also called 'joining of the three yins', as it concerns the three yin organs: the liver, the spleen and the kidneys. It strengthens longevity.

POINT No. 2

St36

Zu San Li

LEG THREE MILES

For a stronger body

LOCATION

Measure four finger widths below the kneecap and one finger width to the outside of the shinbone, the middle finger touching the tibial crest. The point can be found in the depression you can feel when vigorously massaging the area (depending on the point's sensitivity to pressure).

PRESSURE POINT St36: OVERVIEW

CORRESPONDING AREA

Abdomen

ENERGY FUNCTIONS

- Regulates the stomach, strengthens the spleen and transforms humidity
- Invigorates qi and yang, nourishes the blood and yin
- Calms Shen
- Stimulates the meridian and relieves pain
- Reinvigorates yang and restores consciousness

INDICATIONS

- Fatigue, exhaustion, convalescence
- Dyspnoea
- Coughs
- Digestive disorders, epigastric pain, vomiting, belching, distension and pain in the stomach, flatulence, diarrhoea
- Oedema
- Hypertension
- Dizziness, loss of consciousness
- Fever, shivering
- Manic-depressive state
- Painful obstruction in the throat
- Swelling in the breast
- Pains, mobility disorders of the lower limbs

AN EXTRA TIP

Point **St36** is the principal point in preventing diseases, preserving health and extending life. Work on it regularly, starting from the age of 35. Once a week, massage the point for 10 minutes, then stimulate it with moxibustion for 5 to 10 minutes on each leg.

POINT No. 3

UB40

Wei Zhong

SUPPORTING MIDDLE

Master of the lumbar region

LOCATION

Behind the knee, at the centre of the hollow. Locate the point with the knee slightly bent (you can feel a pulsation).

PRESSURE POINT UB40: OVERVIEW

CORRESPONDING AREAS

Lumbar region, back

ENERGY FUNCTIONS

- Regulates the lumbar region
- Acts on the back
- Relieves the knees
- Has a beneficial effect on the bladder
- Stimulates the meridian and relieves pain
- Cools the blood
- Unblocks the meridians

INDICATIONS

- Pain and stiffness in the lumbar spine
- Heaviness in the lumbar region and buttocks
- Pain in the knee
- Pain in the legs
- Pain and cramps in the calf
- Pain in the vertebral column
- Pain in the hip joint
- Sciatica, back pain
- Weakness in the legs
- Haemorrhoid pain
- Sunstroke
- Dysentery disorders
- Eczema, skin rash
- Simultaneous vomiting and diarrhoea
- Malaria

SOME EXTRA TIPS

- You can massage this point regularly to promote the free movement of qi and blood in the lumbar region and, by extension, in the back. Use the dispersion method to massage the area, never the tonification method (see page 24).
- Never apply moxibustion on this point: it damages the artery and the popliteal vein and causes heat in the blood.

POINT No. 4

GB30

Huan Tiao

JUMPING CIRCLE

For the lower limbs

LOCATION

The point is located on the line connecting the sacral hiatus (the opening into the verterbral canal – feel for the bone located at the top of the buttock cleft) and the greater trochanter (top of the femur, at the outer fold of the buttock), two-thirds of the way along. It's more easily located when you lie on your side, flexing the leg of the side to be stimulated.

PRESSURE POINT GB30: OVERVIEW

CORRESPONDING AREAS

Thighs, legs

ENERGY FUNCTIONS

- Opens the principal meridian and Luo meridians of communication (networks that branch off from the vertical channels)
- Relieves pain
- Has beneficial effects on the hip joint and leg
- Eliminates wind-humidity
- Strengthens the tendons and the joints
- Invigorates qi and the blood

INDICATIONS

- Pain in the buttocks
- Pain in the lumbar and lumbosacral regions
- Mobility disorders of the lower limbs
- Pain in the hip, sciatica
- Inability to bend or stretch the knee
- Contracture and pain in the thigh
- Atrophy and paraesthesia (pins and needles) of the lower limb
- Hemiplegia (paralysis of one side of the body), paralysis

AN EXTRA TIP

With regular massage, this point helps stimulate qi and the blood in the lower limbs, maintaining good mobility.

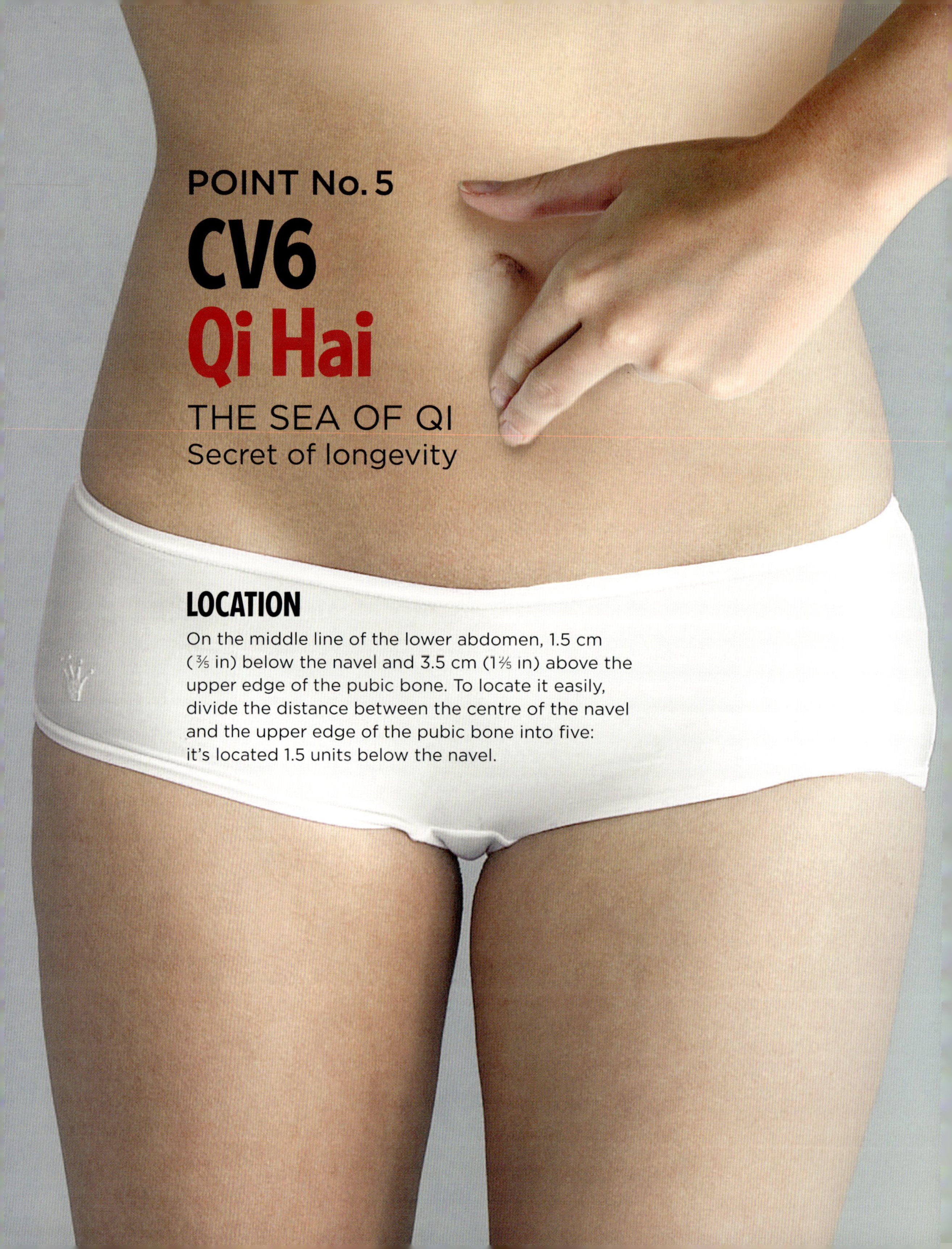

POINT No. 5

CV6

Qi Hai

THE SEA OF QI

Secret of longevity

LOCATION

On the middle line of the lower abdomen, 1.5 cm (3/5 in) below the navel and 3.5 cm (1 2/5 in) above the upper edge of the pubic bone. To locate it easily, divide the distance between the centre of the navel and the upper edge of the pubic bone into five: it's located 1.5 units below the navel.

PRESSURE POINT CV6: OVERVIEW

CORRESPONDING AREAS

Immune system, yang-qi

ENERGY FUNCTIONS

- Maintains your original qi
- Invigorates and strongly raises qi
- Invigorates the kidney, strengthens yang and retains qi
- Saves a collapsing yang (reactivation by moxibustion)
- Energizes qi and harmonizes the blood

INDICATIONS

- Imbalances in the urinary, reproductive, digestive and respiratory systems
- Loss of consciousness
- Asthma, dyspnoea, asthmatic bronchitis
- Gynaecological and obstetric disorders, irregular periods
- Sexual dysfunction for men
- Prostatitis
- Pelvic organ prolapse

SOME EXTRA TIPS

- This point is ideal for treating and preventing states of exhaustion, and for convalescence and maintaining good health. Treat it with moxibustion twice a week for 3 months, for 5 to 10 minutes, until the point becomes red. You can also heat the point before the change of seasons, in combination with **St36**, for optimum health benefits.
- **Please note**: stimulation of this point is prohibited from the third month of pregnancy.

POINT No. 6

LI4

He Gu

JOINING VALLEY

For pain relief

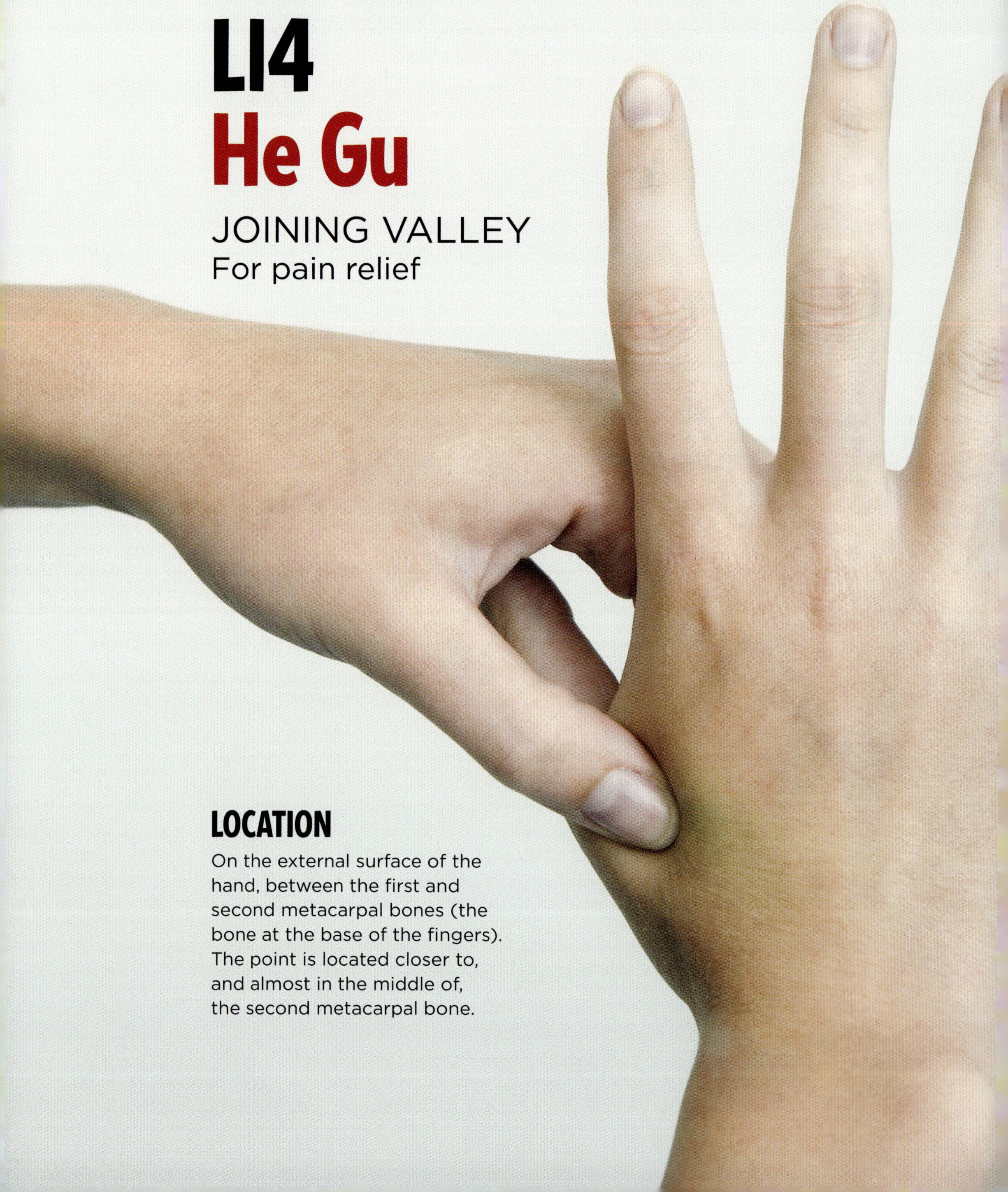

LOCATION

On the external surface of the hand, between the first and second metacarpal bones (the bone at the base of the fingers). The point is located closer to, and almost in the middle of, the second metacarpal bone.

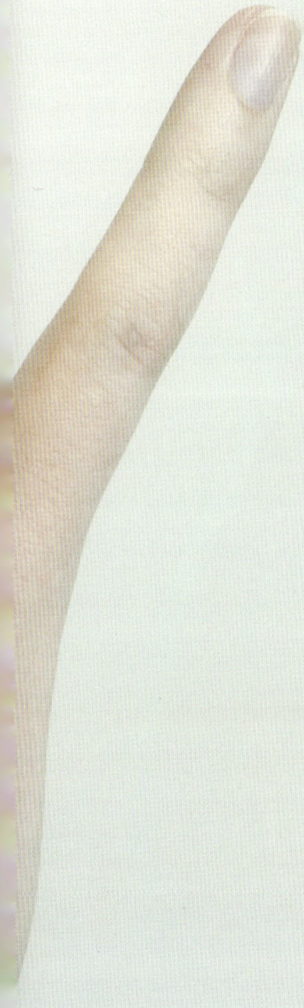

PRESSURE POINT LI4: OVERVIEW

CORRESPONDING AREAS

Face, mouth, nose

ENERGY FUNCTIONS

- Regulates the face and the head, the nose-mouth-ear trio
- Regulates Protective Qi (Wei Qi) and perspiration
- Expels wind and frees the area
- Relieves pain
- Induces labour
- Restores yang

INDICATIONS

- Headache, migraine, hypertension, dizziness
- Nasal congestion, runny nose, rhinitis
- Toothache or pain from a dental cavity
- Painful obstruction in the throat, loss of voice
- Fever, shivers
- Profuse perspiration or absence of perspiration
- Distortion in the face or the mouth
- Pain in the four limbs
- Finger contractures
- Period pains
- Labour

AN EXTRA TIP

This is one of the most frequently used points in clinical practice, and is an extremely important analgesic point (painkiller) for the entire body, especially for disorders relating to the face and sensory organs.

CAUTION!

Stimulation of this point is strictly prohibited for pregnant women, as it may cause miscarriage.

POINT No. 7

P6

Nei Guan

THE INNER GATE

For freeing obstructions

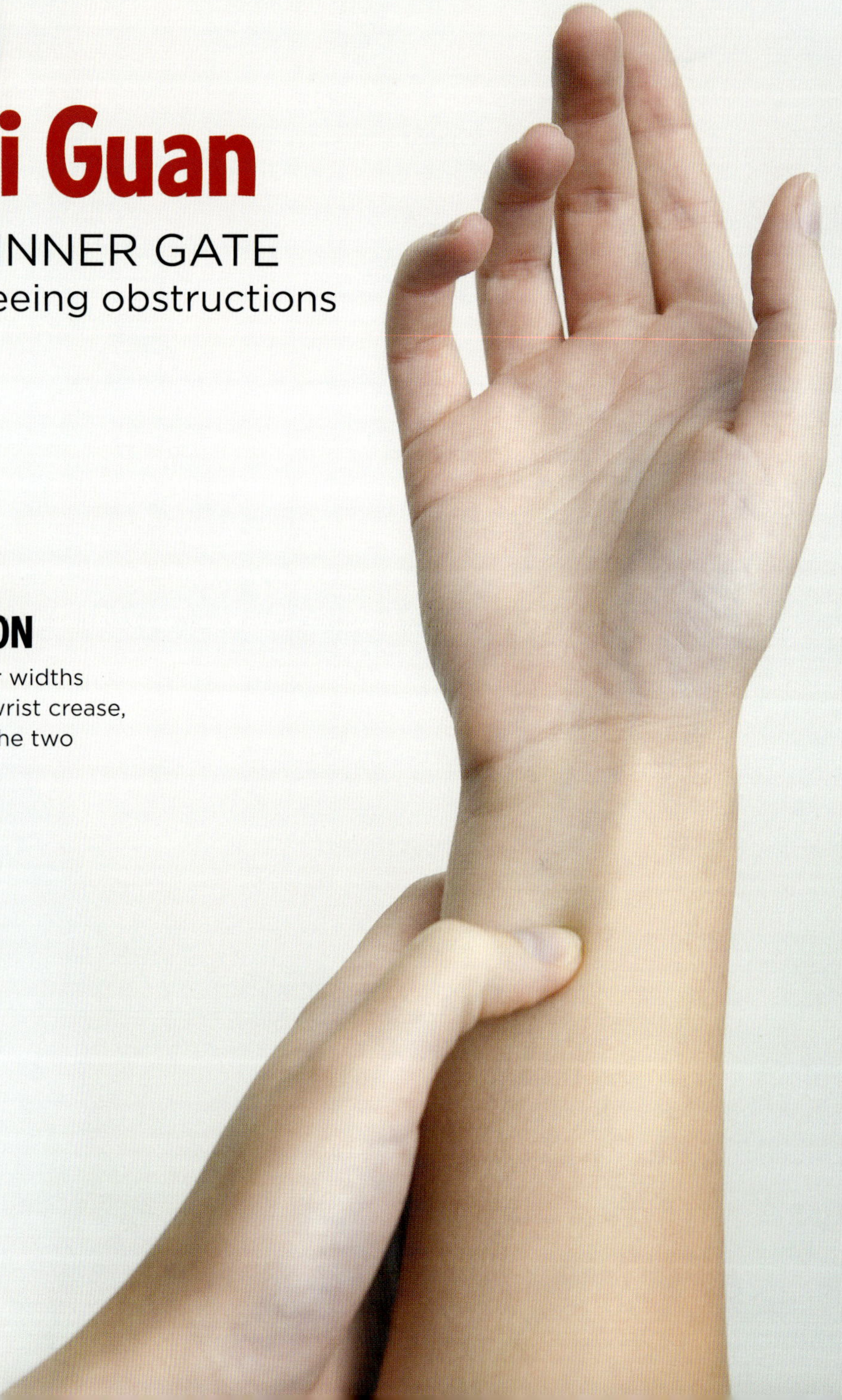

LOCATION

Two finger widths from the wrist crease, between the two tendons.

PRESSURE POINT P6: OVERVIEW

CORRESPONDING AREAS

Heart, chest

ENERGY FUNCTIONS

- Opens the chest and thorax; regulates qi
- Harmonizes the heart and calms Shen
- Harmonizes the stomach
- Clears heat

INDICATIONS

- Pain in the heart, palpitations and irregular heart beat
- Nausea, vomiting and hiccups
- Pain in the lateral rib area
- Insomnia and manic or depressive states
- Hypertension and hypotension
- Gastric and abdominal pain
- Headaches
- Irregular menstrual periods
- Pain and contracture of the elbow and upper arm
- Swelling of the armpit
- Red eyes and red face with hot skin

AN EXTRA TIP

An excellent anti-ageing point, **P6** is also a preventative pressure point promoting longer life. Massaging this point for 5 minutes a day helps to regulate cardiovascular circulation, improve circulation in the thoracic and flank areas and maintain calmness of Shen.

POINT No. 8

Lu7

Lie Que

BROKEN SEQUENCE

To invigorate the lungs

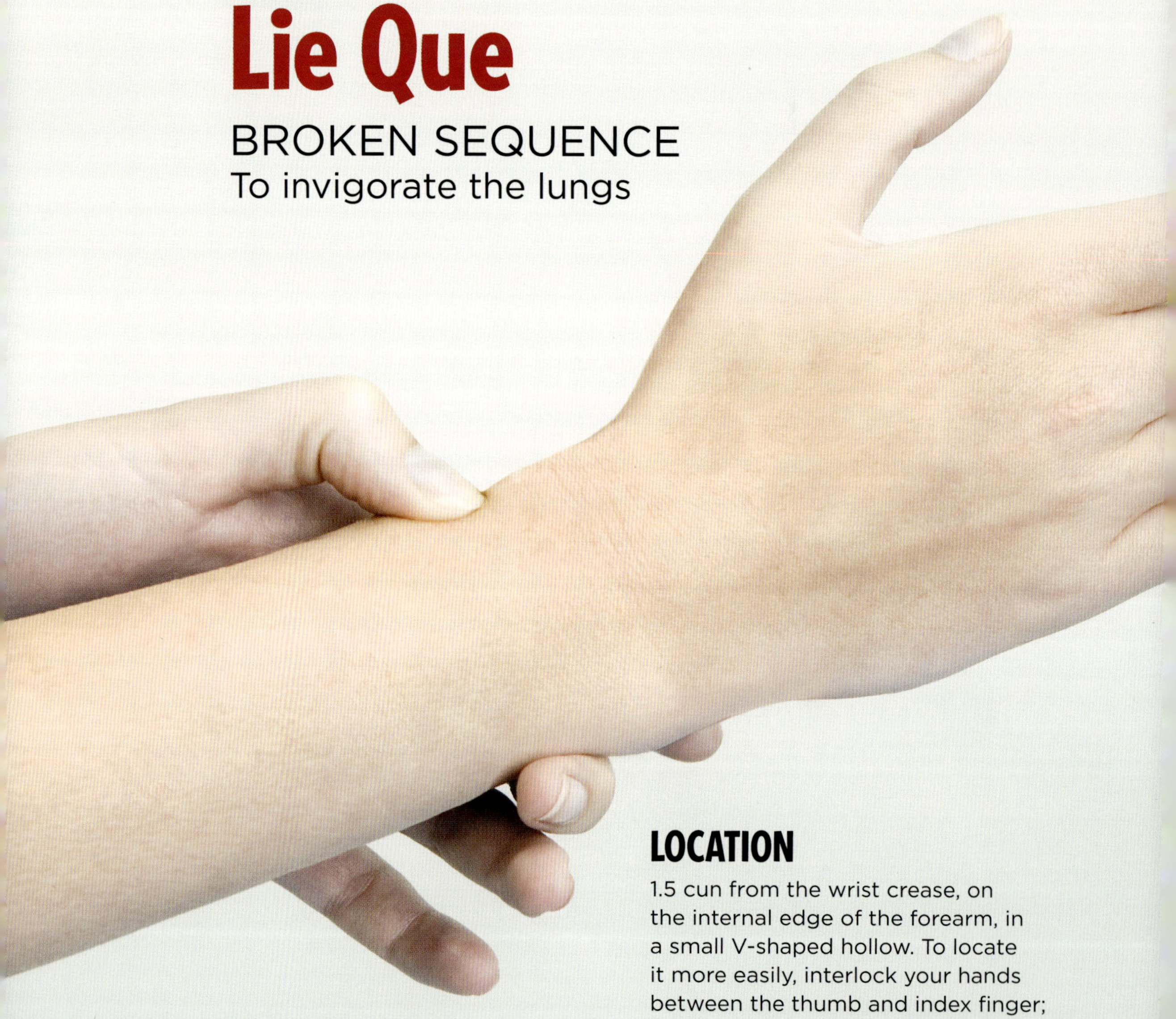

LOCATION

1.5 cun from the wrist crease, on the internal edge of the forearm, in a small V-shaped hollow. To locate it more easily, interlock your hands between the thumb and index finger; the point lies in a small depression located on the edge of the wrist under the tip of your index finger.

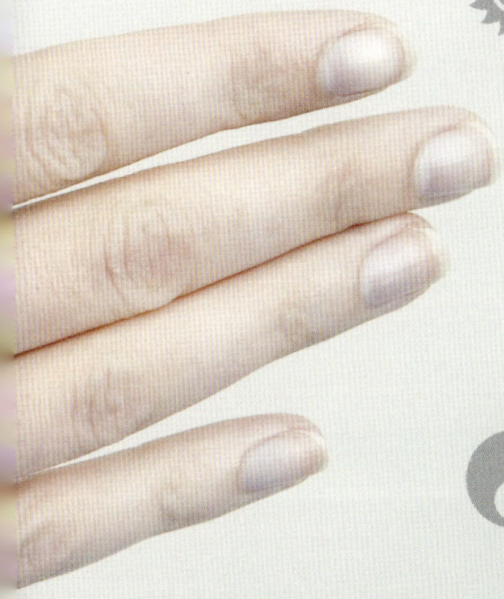

PRESSURE POINT Lu7: OVERVIEW

CORRESPONDING AREAS
Head, nape of the neck

ENERGY FUNCTIONS
- Has beneficial effects on the head and the nape of the neck
- Releases the exterior, expels wind, lowers the lung's qi
- Opens and regulates the Conception Vessel (Ren Mai)
- Regulates the water passages
- Opens the Luo meridians of communication
- Relieves pain

INDICATIONS
- Fever, shivering, cough
- Nasal congestion, runny nose, sinusitis
- Painful obstruction in the throat
- Oedema in the limbs
- Headache, migraine, stiffness in the neck and nape of neck
- Irregularities in the mouth and eyes
- Weakness or pain in the wrist, thumb and hands
- Pain in the shoulder, heat in the hands
- Pain in the genital organs and urinary disorders

AN EXTRA TIP
Massaging this point regularly helps to regulate emotional tensions resulting from worry, sadness and grief, and boosts defensive energy, protecting against viruses and colds.

POINT No. 9

TB6
Zhi Gou

BRANCHING DITCH

The point of the sides

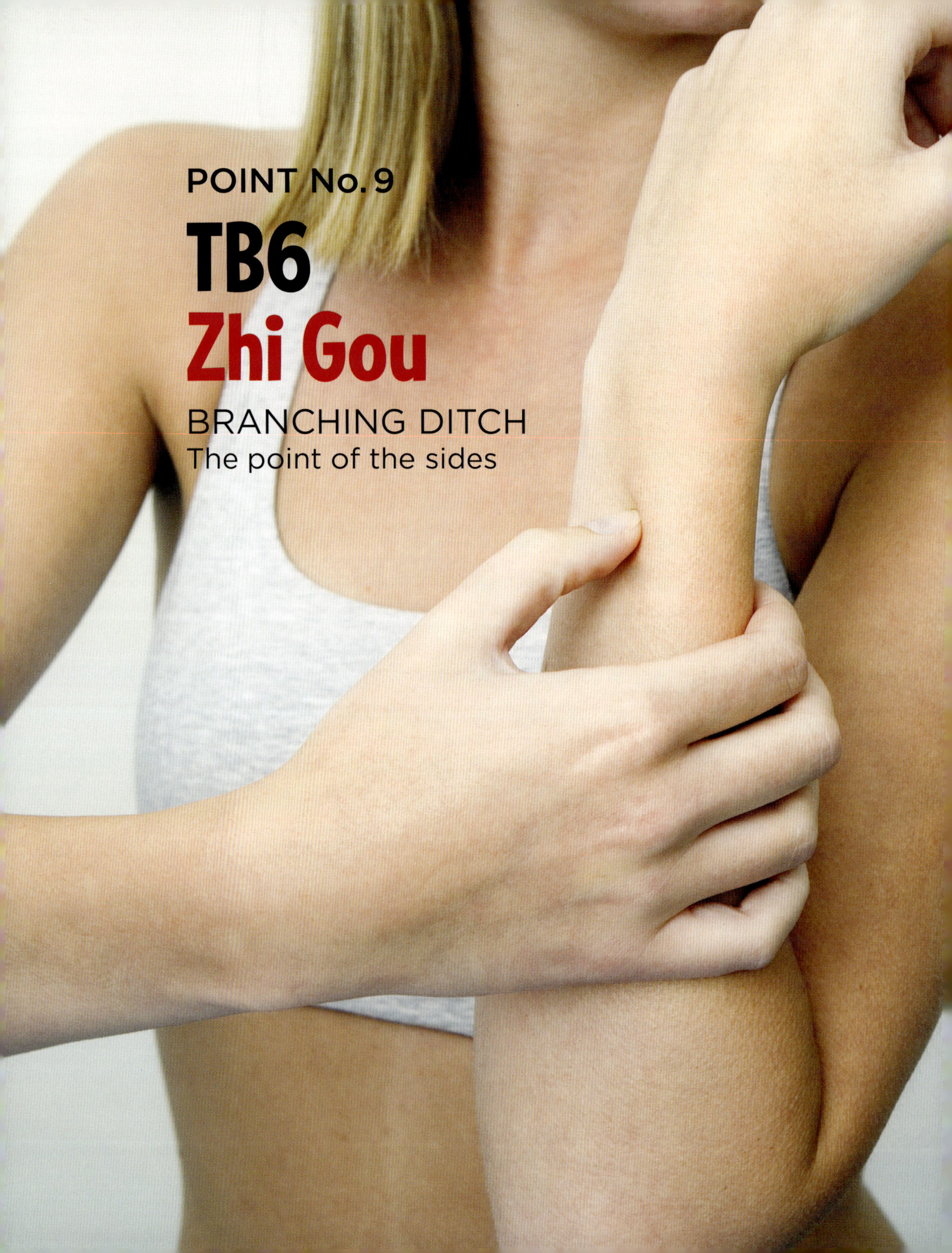

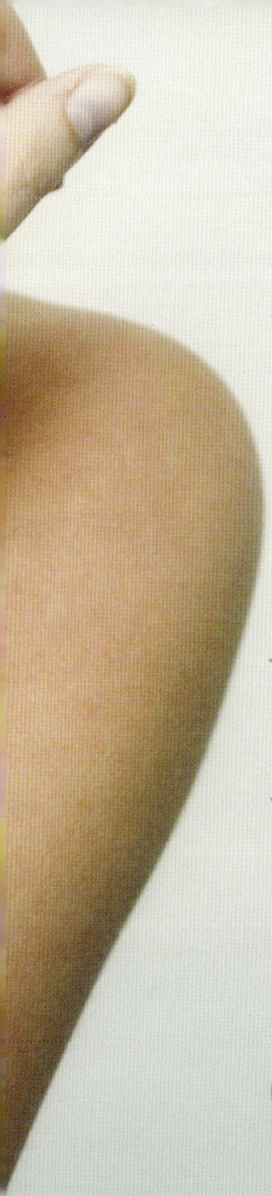

LOCATION

3 cm (1⅕ in) from the wrist crease, in the hollow formed between the radius and the ulna (the two bones in the forearm). **Tip**: It's easier to feel the joint space if you move your wrist.

PRESSURE POINT TB6: OVERVIEW

CORRESPONDING AREAS

Lateral sides of the thorax, flanks

ENERGY FUNCTIONS

- Regulates qi and eliminates the heat of the Triple Burner
- Benefits the lateral areas of the ribs
- Eases movement in the meridians and calms pain
- Promotes bowel function
- Has beneficial effects on the voice

INDICATIONS

- Pain in the lateral areas of the thorax
- Hemiplegia, intercostal neuralgia
- Pain in the shoulder, back, elbow
- Hand numbness, trembling
- Constipation
- Febrile disease with absence of perspiration
- Ear disorders (tinnitus, deafness, sudden loss of voice)
- Redness and pain in the eyes, swelling and pain in the throat
- Coughing with redness and heat in the face

POINT No. 10

LI20

Ying Xiang

WELCOME FRAGRANCE

The nose's ally

LOCATION

At the base of the nostril, in the nasolabial fold (the fold descending from the nostrils). The fold is easier to see when you smile.

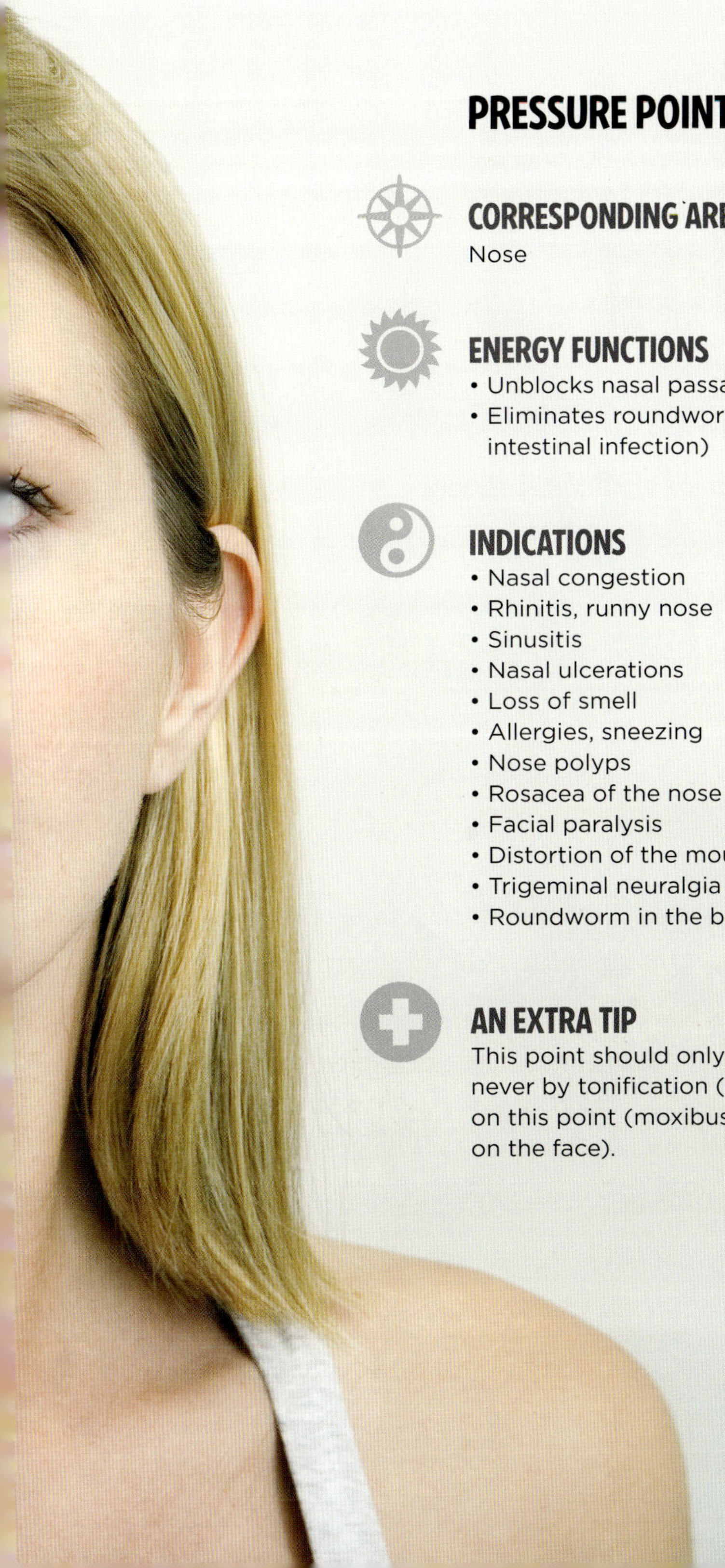

PRESSURE POINT LI20: OVERVIEW

CORRESPONDING AREA

Nose

ENERGY FUNCTIONS

- Unblocks nasal passages
- Eliminates roundworm (parasite causing intestinal infection)

INDICATIONS

- Nasal congestion
- Rhinitis, runny nose
- Sinusitis
- Nasal ulcerations
- Loss of smell
- Allergies, sneezing
- Nose polyps
- Rosacea of the nose
- Facial paralysis
- Distortion of the mouth
- Trigeminal neuralgia
- Roundworm in the bile ducts

AN EXTRA TIP

This point should only be stimulated by dispersion – never by tonification (see page 24). Never use moxa on this point (moxibustion is generally prohibited on the face).

POINT No. 11

GV26

Ren Zhong

MAN'S MIDDLE

The emergency point

LOCATION

In the middle of the indented fold, between the base of the nose and the top of the upper lip.

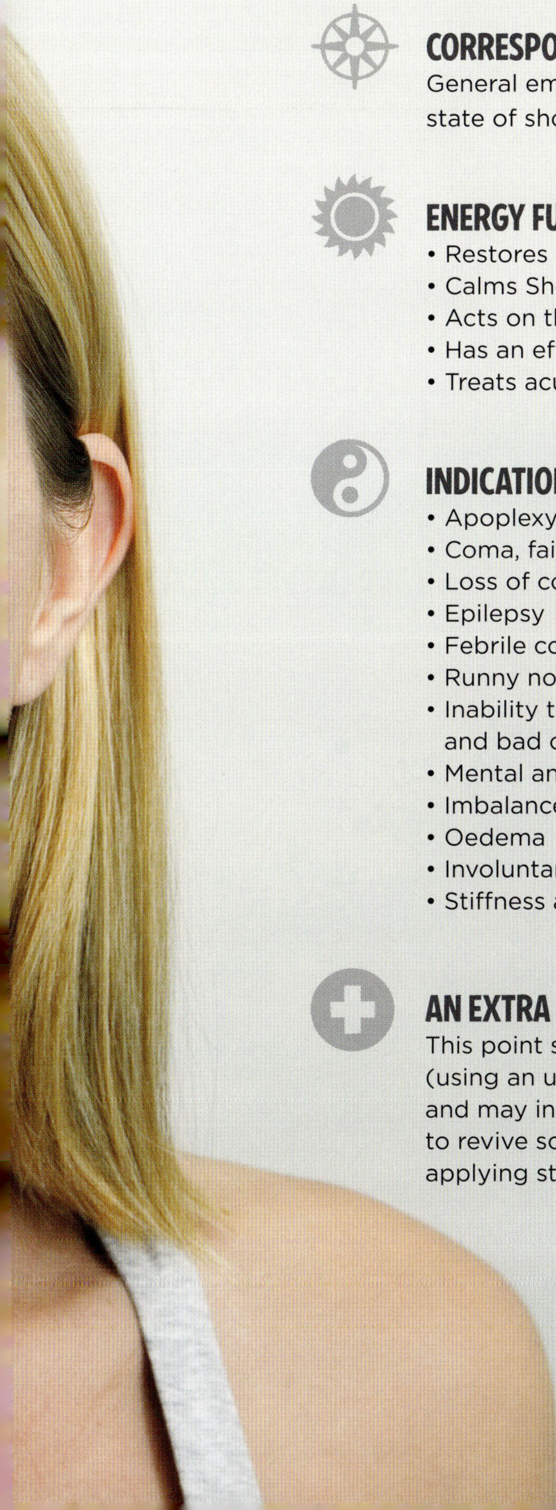

PRESSURE POINT GV26: OVERVIEW

CORRESPONDING AREA

General emergency cases (loss of consciousness, state of shock)

ENERGY FUNCTIONS

- Restores consciousness, wakes Shen
- Calms Shen
- Acts on the face
- Has an effect on the spine
- Treats acute lumbago

INDICATIONS

- Apoplexy
- Coma, fainting, blackout
- Loss of consciousness
- Epilepsy
- Febrile convulsions
- Runny nose
- Inability to differentiate between good and bad odours
- Mental and psychosomatic disorders
- Imbalance from manic depression
- Oedema
- Involuntary laughing and crying
- Stiffness and pain in the spine

AN EXTRA TIP

This point should be stimulated at an oblique angle (using an upward movement). It is very sensitive, and may induce tears. In China, it is commonly used to revive someone experiencing an epileptic fit, by applying strong pressure on the point using a finger.

POINT No. 12

GV20
Bai Hui

HUNDRED MEETINGS
The point of yang

LOCATION
Place your hands on either side of your head, with your thumbs on the top of your ears. Join your index fingers on the top of your head, on the median line. The point lies in a light depression where your fingertips meet, and is sensitive to pressure.

PRESSURE POINT GV20: OVERVIEW

CORRESPONDING AREAS

Head, vertex (top of the skull), Shen

ENERGY FUNCTIONS

- Nourishes the brain, calms Shen
- Pacifies the emotions
- Calms convulsions
- Acts on the head and sense organs
- Raises and/or lowers yang
- Invigorates qi
- Restores yang in great states of exhaustion

INDICATIONS

- Loss of consciousness
- Mental disorders
- Spasms, epilepsy
- Dizziness, headaches, fainting
- Poor memory, lack of intellectual dynamism
- Hemiplegia and aphasia (impaired ability to speak)
- Insomnia
- Dementia
- Tinnitus
- Hypertension, hypotension
- Blocked nose, runny nose
- Ptosis (drooping of the upper eyelid) and prolapse (organs, tissues)
- Hair loss, numbness of the scalp, premature grey hair

AN EXTRA TIP

This point has a dual function depending on whether the tonification or dispersion method is being used. It can either dispel excess yang in the head (mental agitation) or raise yang in the head (dizziness).

Massage this point regularly or tap it with two fingers (100 to 200 times): this boosts the blood flow in the brain, regulates the central nervous system, increases intellectual activity and establishes memory.

5

treating common CONDITIONS

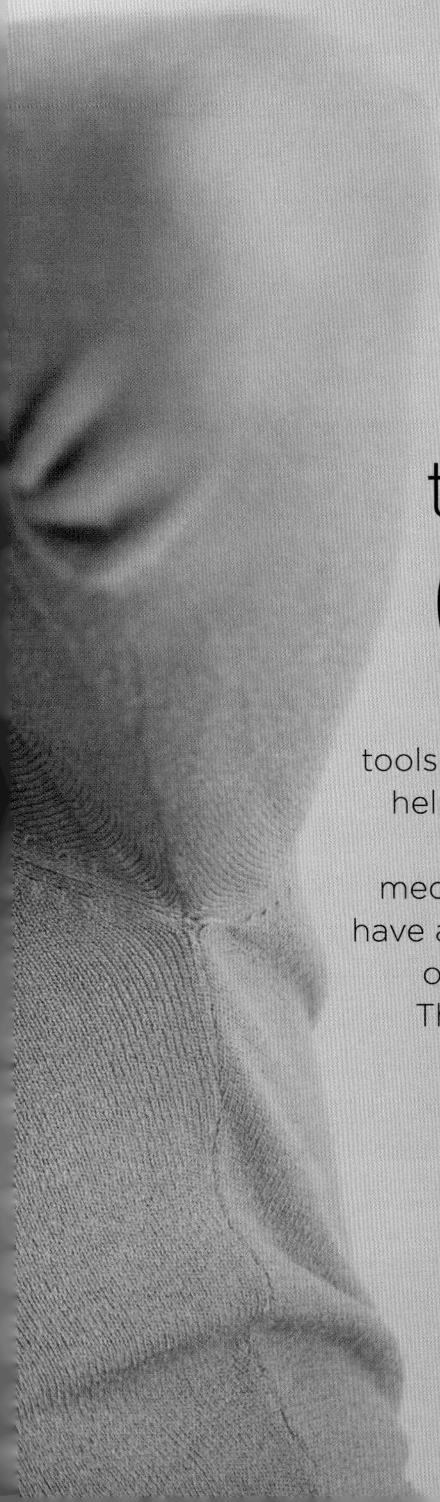

Please note The following pages include tools to guide you along the path to well-being and help you look after your health. The information should not be regarded as personalized medical advice; always consult your doctor if you have any doubts about any aspect of your condition, or wish to seek treatment for any problems. This book should not be used as a substitute for medical treatment.

Bloating & gas

Total duration of treatment:
12 MINUTES

Intestinal disorders are very common and can take many forms: a sensation of 'always being aware of your stomach', bloating, gas, spasmodic pains, abdominal distension, flatulence, problems with bowel movement, chronic inflammation of the colon, alternating constipation and diarrhoea, bad breath ... The causes, however, can be varied – often food intolerances (gluten/lactose), but also psychological disorders, stress, obsessive neuroses, OCD, as well as the use of certain medications.

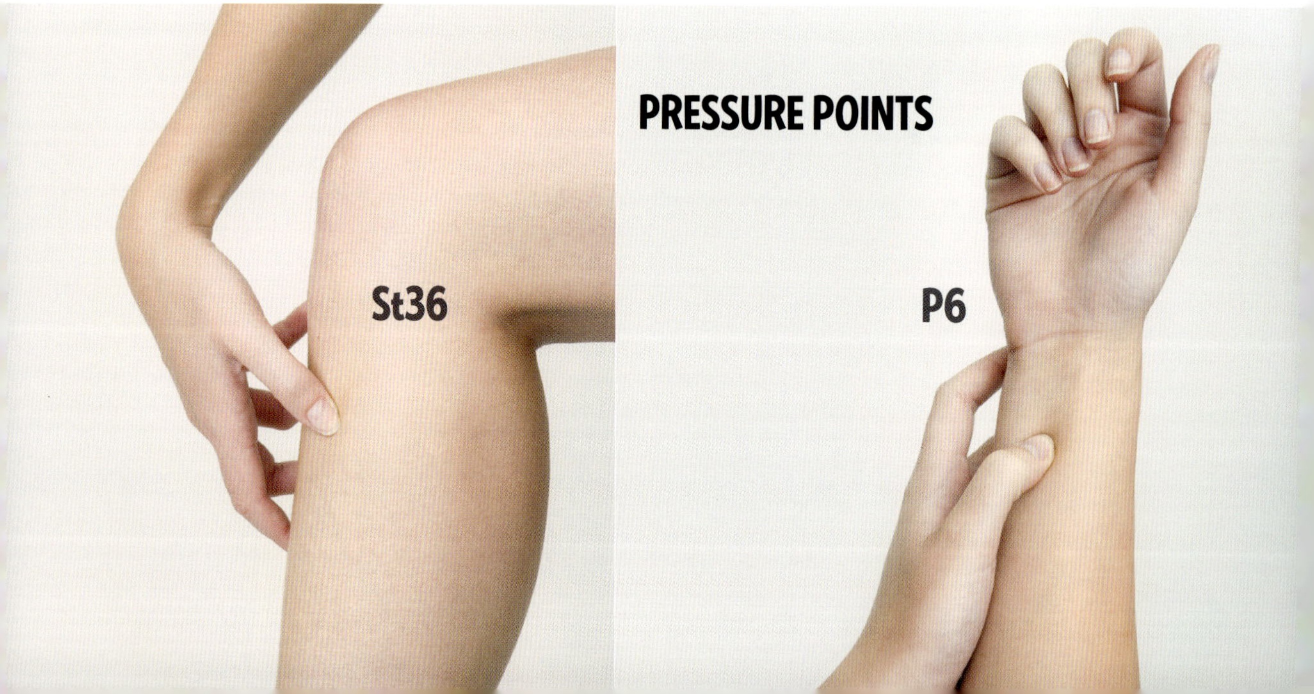

METHOD

Apply moderate pressure to each point with your thumb. Maintain this for 2 minutes, then repeat the procedure on the opposite side.

SOME EXTRA TIPS

- Massage your stomach with 1 or 2 drops of **peppermint essential oil**, in a clockwise direction.
- Opt for **blond psyllium** (from organic food shops), effective in regulating bowel movements: dilute 1 tablespoon in a glass of water and drink it before meals.
- Try **chamomile herbal tea**, antispasmodics and probiotics (from pharmacies) to preserve intestinal flora.

IN TRADITIONAL CHINESE MEDICINE

There is a close relationship between the liver and the spleen/stomach pairing. Inadequate nutrition and emotional disturbances blocking the liver cause energy to stagnate, creating an imbalance between the liver and the spleen (even though the location is the intestines), because it causes disorders in the movement of energy and regular bowel movements in the intestines. The abdominal pains (spasmodic) come from blockage of the liver's energy. The trigger and development of this imbalance can also be activated by an inadequate lifestyle.

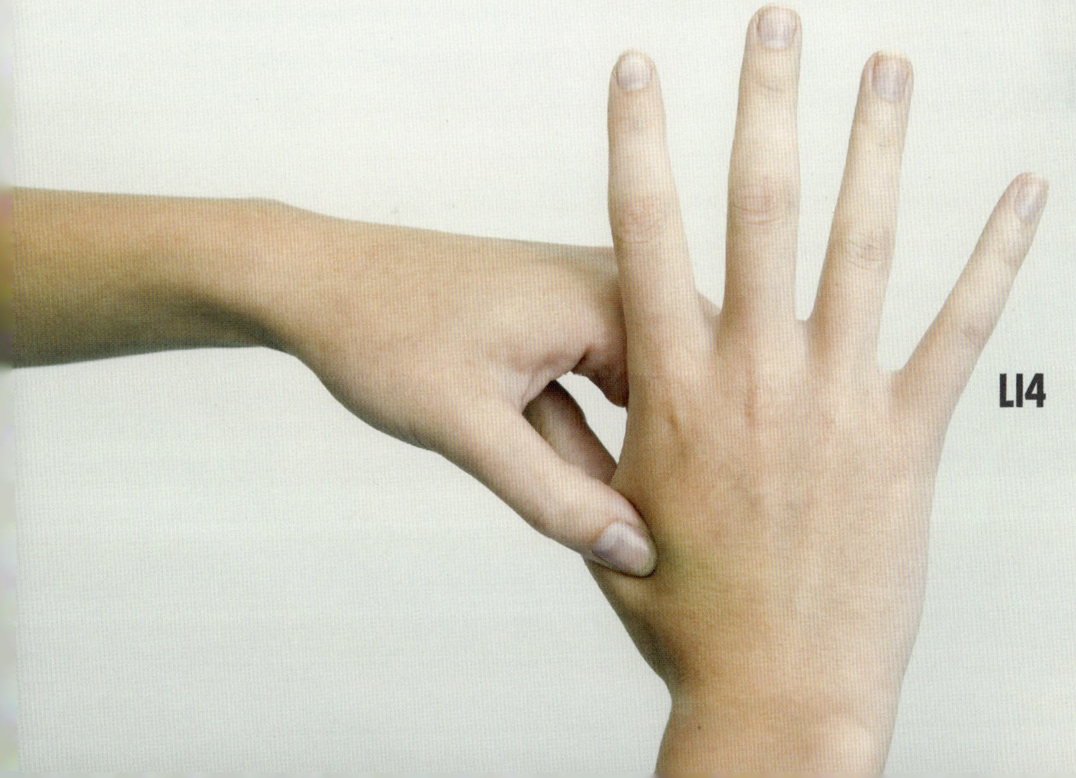

Constipation

Total duration of treatment:
10 MINUTES

Constipation is defined as bowel movements that are difficult to pass or infrequent (fewer than three stools per week). The stools are hard, and include the sensations of bloating and incomplete evacuation.

METHOD

Apply moderate pressure to each point with your thumb. Maintain this for 2 minutes, then repeat the procedure on the opposite side.

PRESSURE POINTS

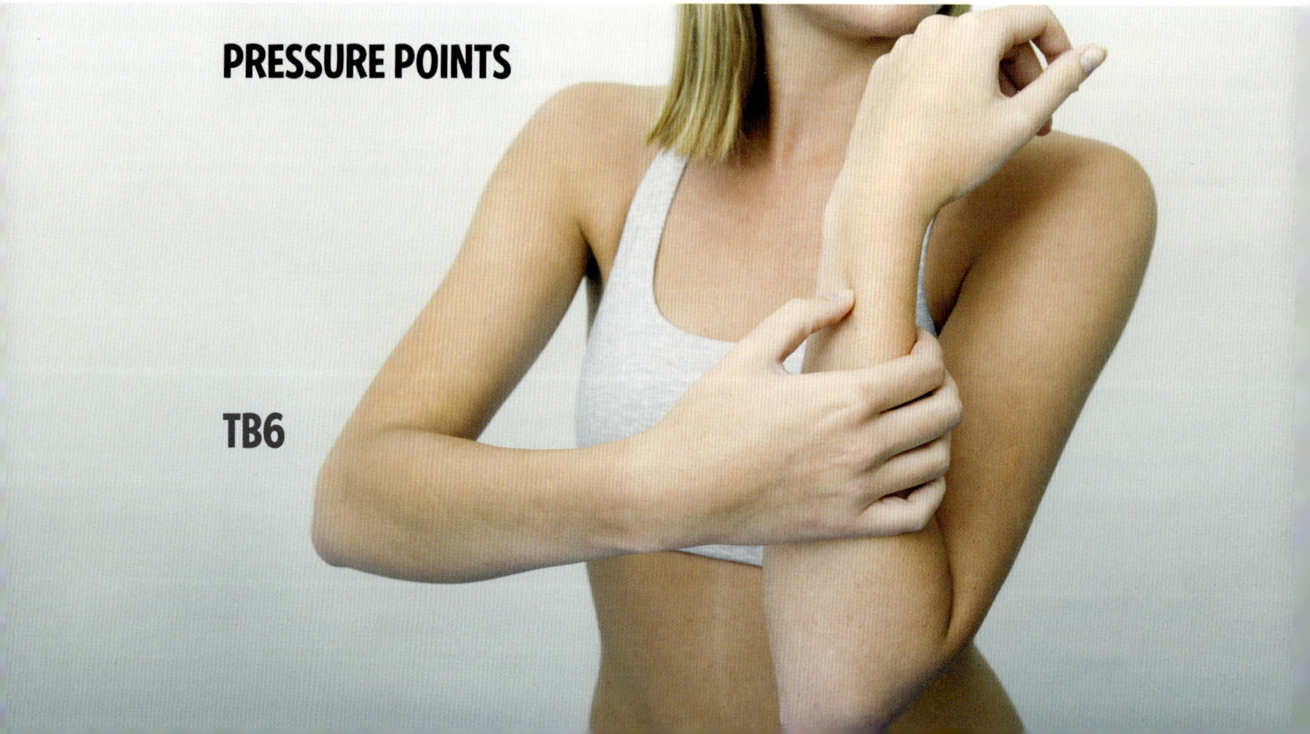

IN TRADITIONAL CHINESE MEDICINE

One or two stools per day is considered to be a normal bowel movement. Anything less frequent than that, however, is regarded as constipation. The main cause is the depletion of liquids, which leads to dryness of the intestines and progressive dehydration from yin deficiency. Four imbalances can cause constipation: cold, heat, deficiency and abundance. Constipation can also be related to chronic illness, leading to loss of energy and insufficient strength to push the stools.

SOME EXTRA TIPS

- Try **blond psyllium**, the best natural regulator of intestinal function (see also page 67).
- Avoid chocolate, processed foods made with white flour (pasta, breads), gluten and dairy. Opt for prebiotics (best consumed raw) to nourish your good intestinal bacteria, such as onions, salsify, asparagus, endives and Jerusalem artichokes.

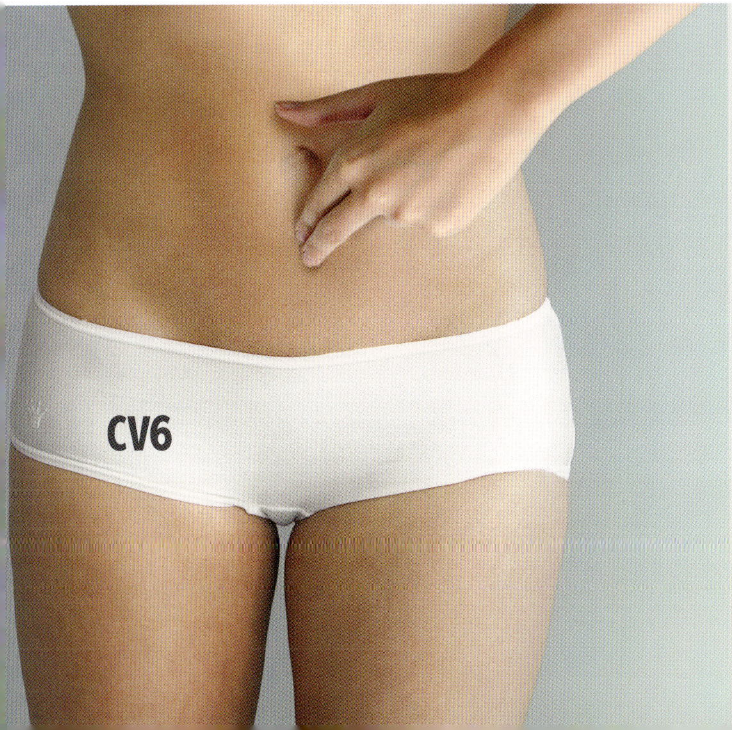

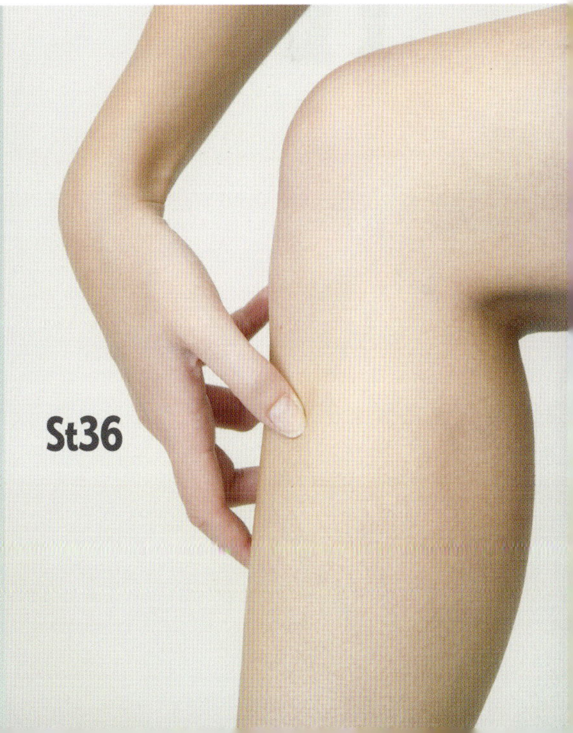

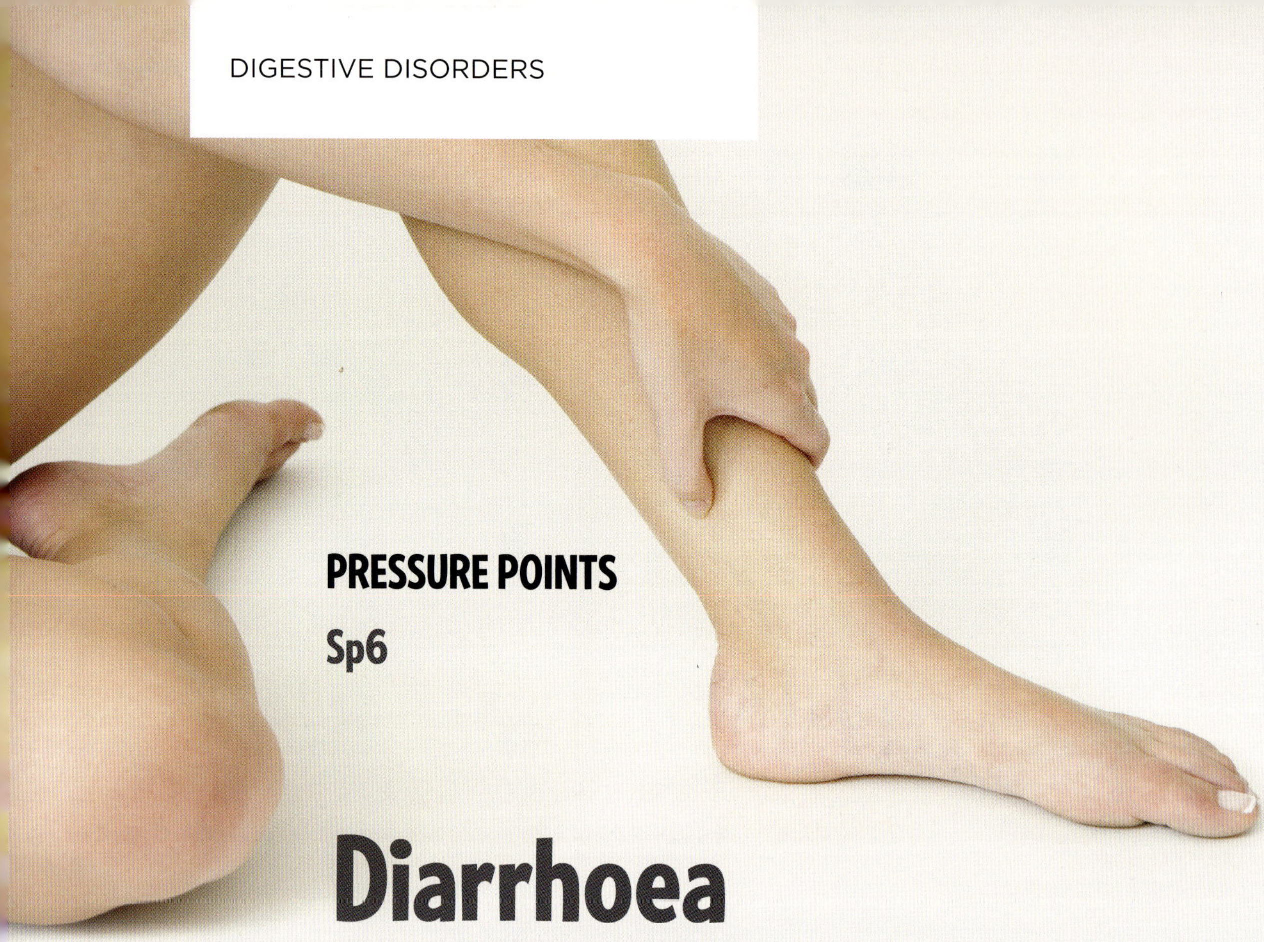

PRESSURE POINTS

Sp6

Diarrhoea

Total duration of treatment:
8 MINUTES

Diarrhoea is defined as having stools that are too abundant, too liquid and/or too frequent. This can be combined with a sensation of cold in the stomach, fatigue, tiredness, bloating and sensitivity to cold.

METHOD

Apply moderate pressure to point **Sp6** with your thumb. Maintain this for 2 minutes, then repeat the procedure on the opposite side. To complement this, heat point **St36** for 2 minutes with a moxa stick (repeat on other side).

IN TRADITIONAL CHINESE MEDICINE

Diarrhoea can be attributed to the retention of cold and the excessive consumption of refrigerated products, ice cream and raw salads. It can also be induced by a surplus of humidity in the body, related to overconsumption of dairy products, or can be linked to an intolerance to gluten. The spleen is suffering from deficiency and the centre must be heated to invigorate energy and stop stools.

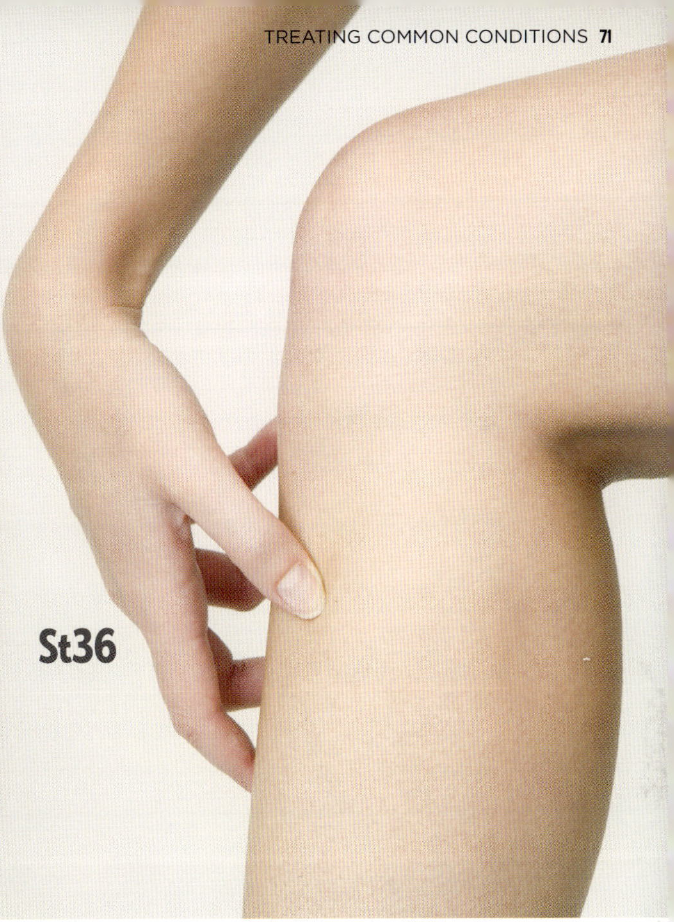

SOME EXTRA TIPS

- Apply 1 drop of **ginger essential oil** (diluted in 1 drop of plant oil) on **St36** before applying heat to the point with moxa. This helps to strengthen the effect of heating and tonification of the spleen.
- Avoid raw and cold foods, which stagnate and attack the spleen's energy, meat and all fatty products, lubricants and laxatives, as well as spicy flavours that harm the spleen. Instead, choose foods that strengthen the spleen, such as apples, chestnuts, lotus seeds, eggs and fish. Also consider carrots and certain warming spices, such as cinnamon, cloves and ginger.

VARIATION

You could also apply heat to the navel and the area around it until the skin becomes red (for about 10 minutes). The heat invigorates the area and helps to stop stools.

Stomach pains

Total duration of treatment:
14 MINUTES

As with bloating and gas, stomach pains can be due to inflammatory, toxic or allergic reasons. They may also be caused by a digestive ulcer, acute or chronic gastric neurosis, gastroptosis (displacement of the stomach) and pancreatitis. This can be accompanied by vomiting and haematemesis (vomiting of blood). Consult your doctor if the signs persist.

PRESSURE POINTS

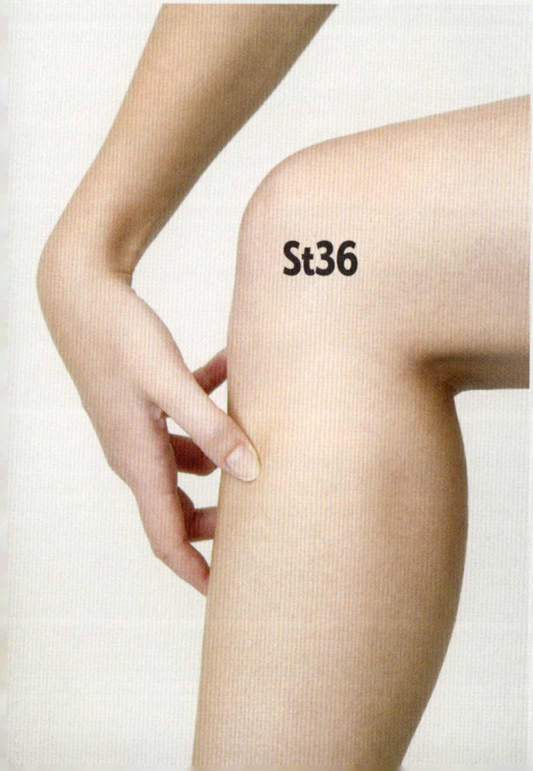

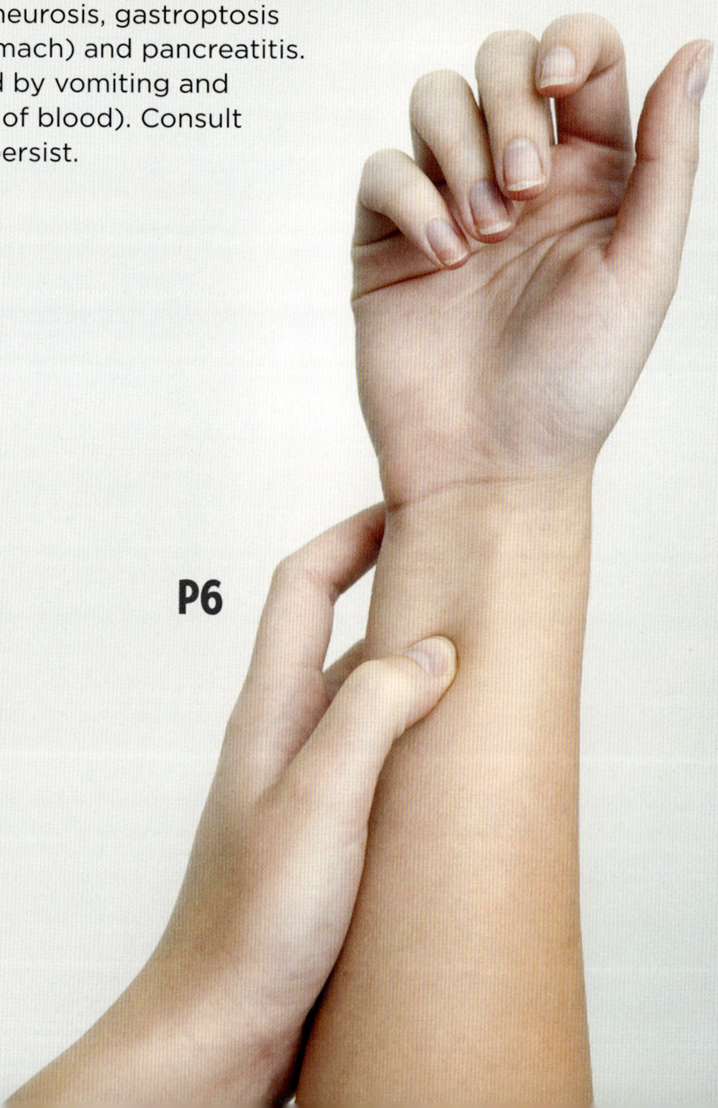

METHOD

Apply moderate pressure to each point with your thumb. Maintain this for 2 minutes, then repeat on the opposite side.

SOME EXTRA TIPS

- **Aloe vera** (gel or juice) relieves the oesophageal wall and is beneficial to the health of the mucous membrane. You could also try probiotics (from the pharmacy), which act on the bacteria causing the imbalance.
- Try eliminating gluten and dairy products from your diet for a minimum of 6 months.

IN TRADITIONAL CHINESE MEDICINE

According to classical Chinese medicine, stomach pains are also linked to the spleen and the liver. They result most often from the obstruction of the stomach's qi induced by cold or heat, or even from the stomach being attacked by the liver's qi, provoked, for example, by emotional disturbances, an uncontrolled diet, an accumulation of humidity and of phlegm ... It's important to unblock the liver's qi, regulate qi and harmonize the stomach to stop the pains. In the long term, these pains could become chronic if there is no change in lifestyle and the emotional disturbances continue.

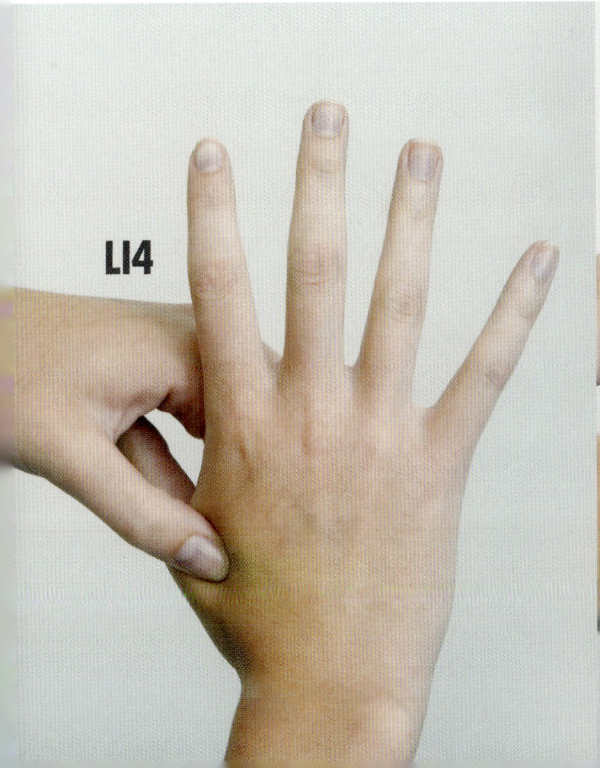

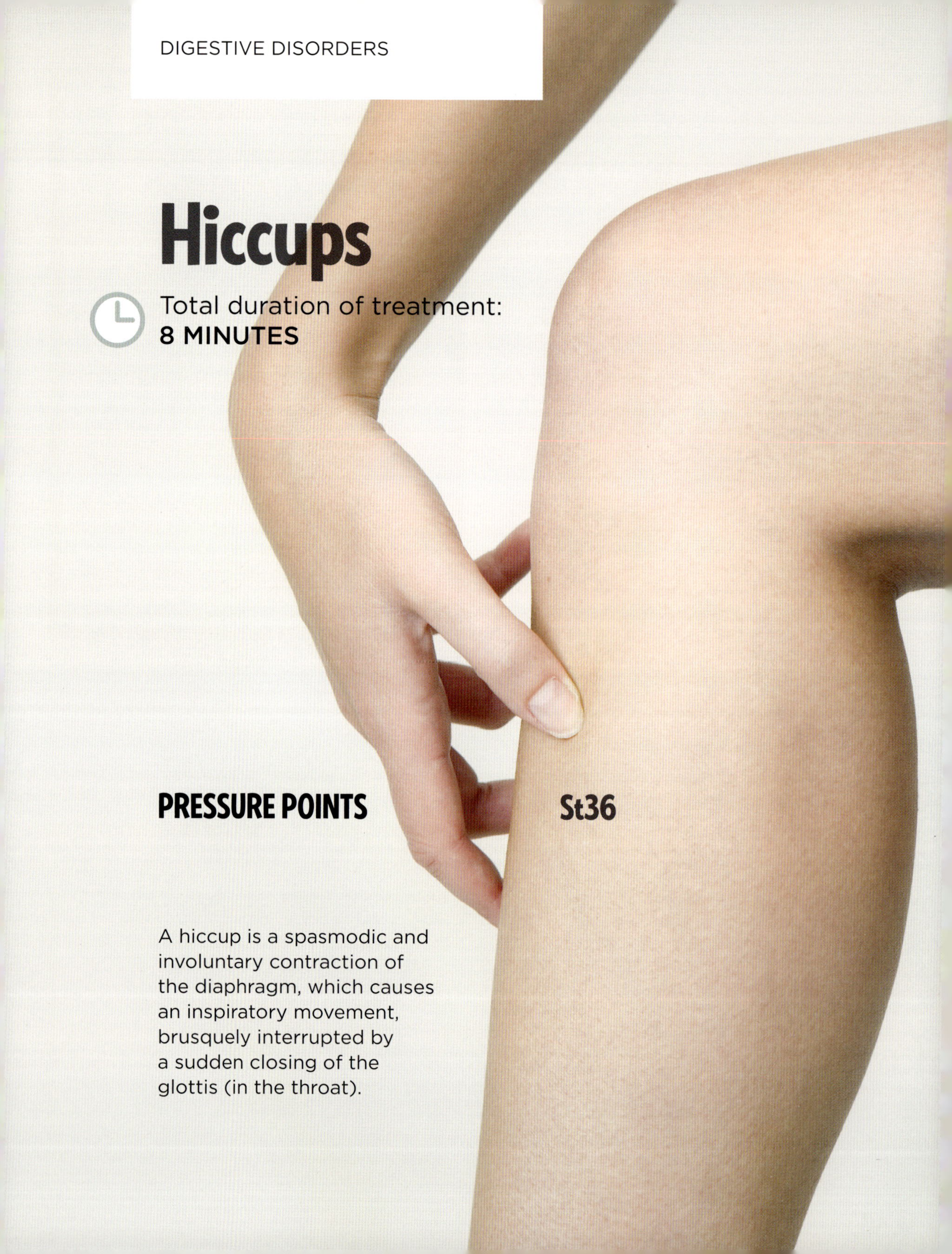

Hiccups

Total duration of treatment:
8 MINUTES

PRESSURE POINTS

St36

A hiccup is a spasmodic and involuntary contraction of the diaphragm, which causes an inspiratory movement, brusquely interrupted by a sudden closing of the glottis (in the throat).

METHOD

Apply moderate pressure to each point with your thumb. Maintain this for 2 minutes, then repeat the procedure on the opposite side.

SOME EXTRA TIPS

- Drink a glass of water quickly while holding your breath. This is a popular trick that actually works. Repeat if necessary.
- You could also apply 1 drop of **tarragon essential oil** on your tongue. But beware: this essential oil is an irritant and stings – the effect of this, however, being such that it stops the hiccups!

IN TRADITIONAL CHINESE MEDICINE

Hiccups do not correspond to a single pathology. This condition is part of a group of imbalances that can correspond to what is commonly known in the West as gastro-oesophageal reflux. This is a complex pathology characterized by a stagnation of the phlegm's qi and a depletion caused by emotional tensions, an unbalanced diet and exhaustion. If the hiccups are very frequent, you may need to consult a specialist.

Motion sickness

Total duration of treatment:
6 MINUTES

Motion sickness is linked to stimulation of the labyrinth, the complex inner ear system made up of intercommunicating cavities and tubes. General discomfort is accompanied by nausea or vomiting and can occur while in any mode of transport: boat, car, airplane or train.

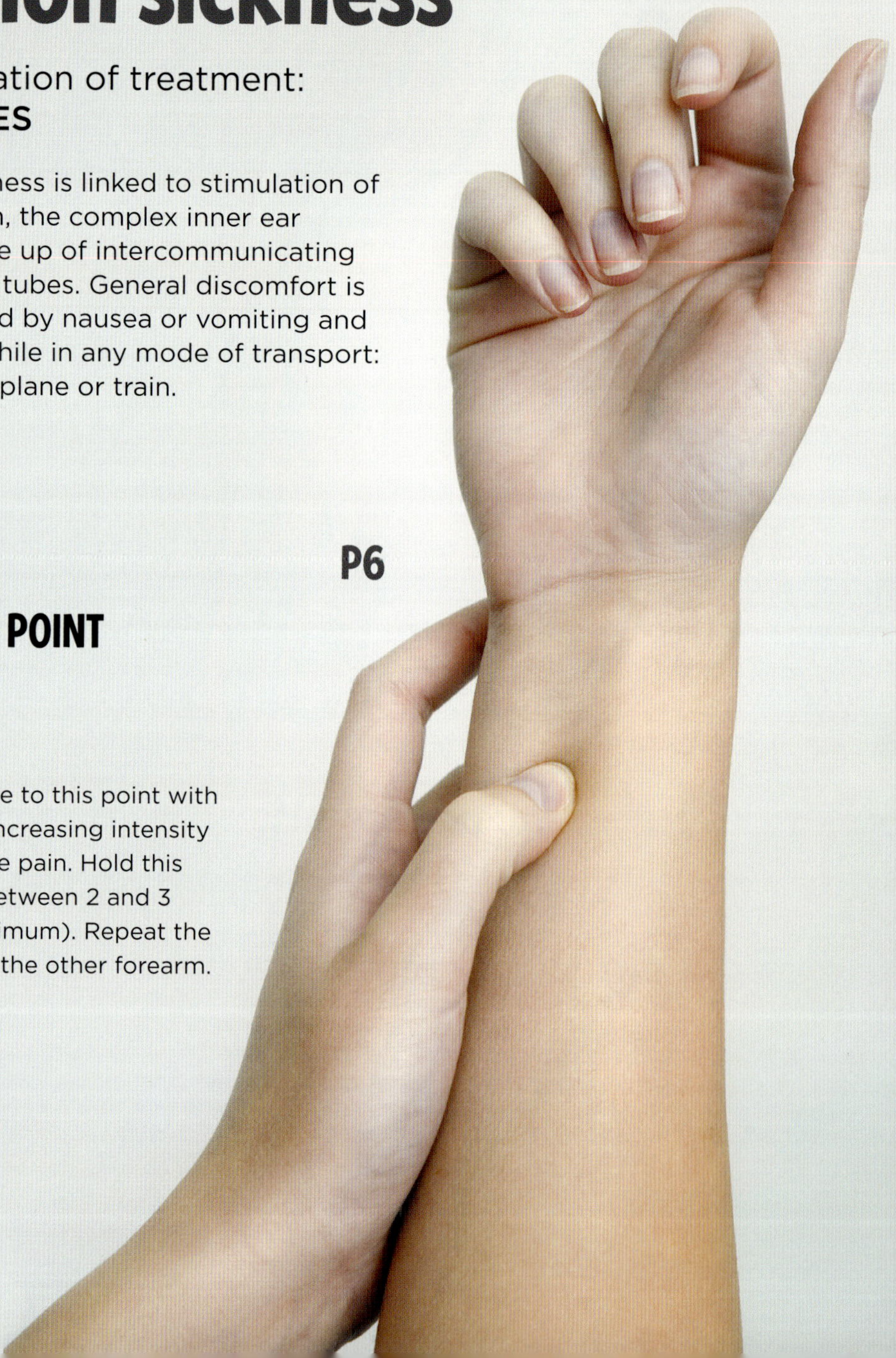

PRESSURE POINT

METHOD

Apply pressure to this point with your thumb, increasing intensity until you sense pain. Hold this position for between 2 and 3 minutes (maximum). Repeat the procedure on the other forearm.

VARIATION

You could also use magnet therapy on the same point (use magnets typically intended for joint pain relief). Place these on the point and turn the tip of the magnet outwards in the direction of the thumb. Attach it with a sticking plaster. Apply it at least half an hour before departure, or during the journey as necessary. Be careful not to exceed three applications within a few hours.

AN EXTRA TIP

Apply 1 or 2 drops of **lavender or peppermint essential oil** onto the wrists and massage this in. If suffering from nausea, you could also apply a drop of **peppermint essential oil** under the tongue.

IN TRADITIONAL CHINESE MEDICINE

This discomfort is, for the most part, linked to disturbances in the liver and the gall bladder. It is thus important to take preventative action relating to this duo.

Nausea & vomiting

Total duration of treatment:
12 MINUTES

The desire to vomit can have various causes, some of which are linked to the nervous system, the stomach and the digestive tract. Most types of nausea are related to stomach flu (gastroenteritis) or food poisoning. Nausea can also be a side effect of many medicines, including chemotherapy medication. If it continues, and is accompanied by vomiting, it could lead to rapid dehydration: this should be treated immediately.

PRESSURE POINTS

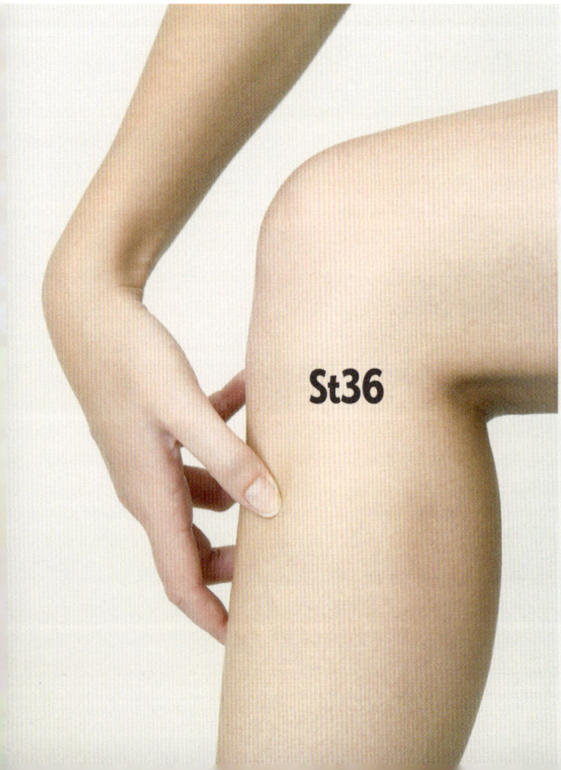

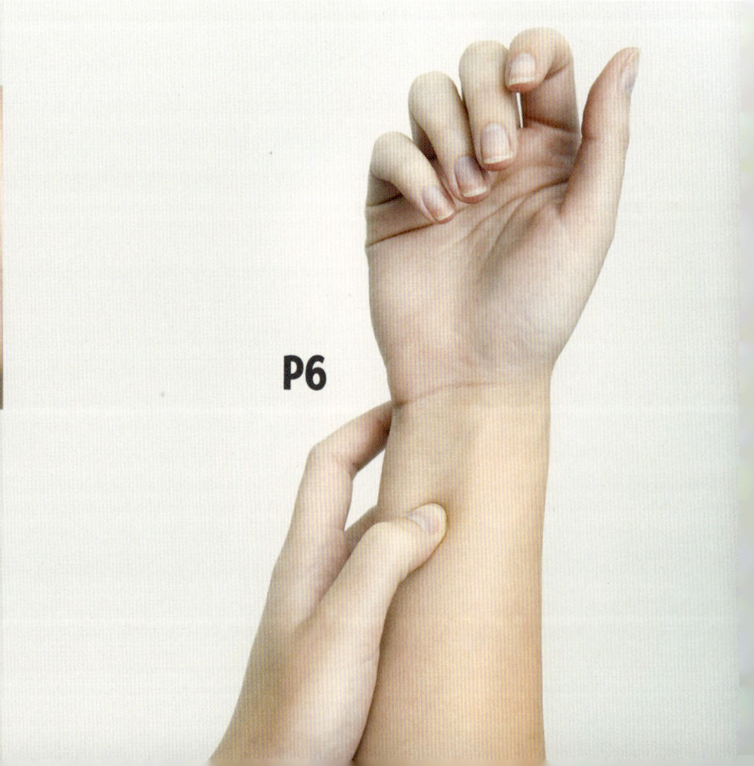

METHOD

Apply moderate pressure to each point with your thumb. Maintain this for 2 minutes, then repeat the procedure on the opposite side.

SOME EXTRA TIPS

- **Fresh ginger** is excellent for settling the stomach. Chew a small piece of fresh ginger or prepare a ginger infusion: chop 2 or 3 long slices of fresh ginger, add it to 200ml (7fl oz) boiling water and let it boil for 5 minutes. Strain, then drink (you can sweeten it with honey, if desired). Repeat until the nausea subsides. This remedy is also effective for morning sickness during pregnancy.
- Alternatively, lick 1 drop of **ginger essential oil** placed on the back of your hand. Repeat up to five times per day maximum.

IN TRADITIONAL CHINESE MEDICINE

The stomach's energy has a downward movement. When this energy cannot descend, it rises against the flow, resulting in nausea and vomiting. Regulating the stomach and the digestive tract is therefore key, the principle being to normalize it and cause the stomach's energy to descend. Stimulation of the energy points is one of the most efficient natural therapeutic techniques, in addition to a healthy diet, which also plays an important role.

Seasonal allergies

Total duration of treatment:
14 MINUTES

An allergy is an excessive and specific reaction from the immune system to attack foreign bodies (see also Strengthening immunity, page 156). It reacts forcefully, producing severe inflammation and creating allergic symptoms. In addition to respiratory symptoms, allergies can manifest as eczema, skin eruptions, digestive disorders, headaches and eye disorders, and affect the ENT passages.

METHOD

- Apply moderate pressure to each point (except **St36**) with your thumb. Maintain this for 2 minutes. Repeat the procedure on the opposite side.
- You could also stimulate point **St36** with a moxa stick for 10 minutes.

PRESSURE POINTS

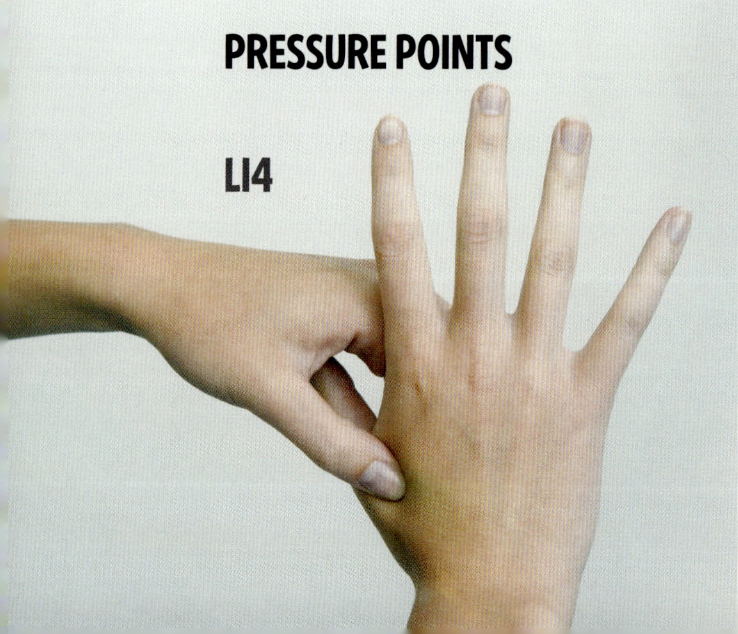

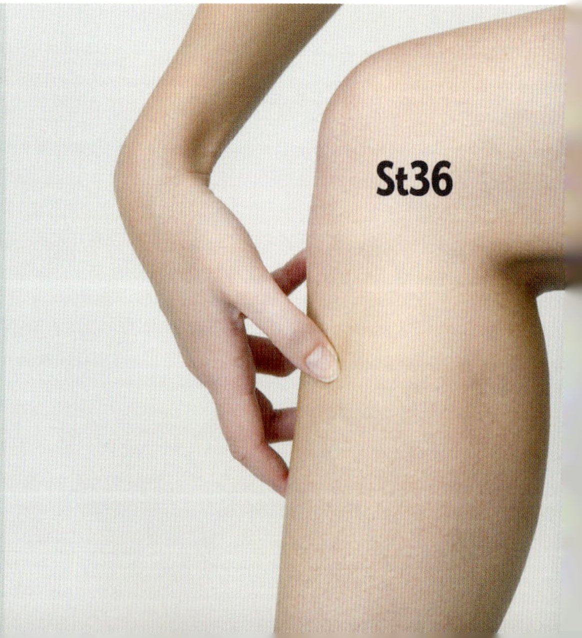

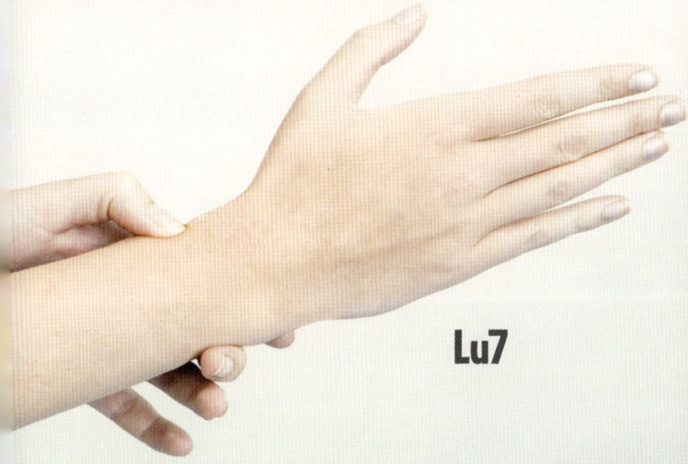

IN TRADITIONAL CHINESE MEDICINE

The immune system relies heavily on the lung network. The lungs are responsible for managing the body's defensive energies, and protect us from foreign bodies as well as nourish the skin. When the lung network isn't properly nourished, or if its energy is weak, the immune system also weakens, leaving the way open to imbalances.

SOME EXTRA TIPS

- Avoid gluten, dairy products and processed foods as much as possible. Favour an organic, fibre-rich diet.
- Opt for **probiotics** (from the pharmacy). They stimulate and balance the intestinal flora, essential in protecting against allergic reactions and regulating inflammation.
- Also consider **fish oils** and **omega-3s** for their anti-inflammatory effects.

VARIATION

For immediate relief if your sinuses are affected: apply moderate pressure with your index finger on point **LI20** (on each side of your nose) for 3 minutes while taking deep and slow breaths. In China, this point is traditionally used to clear a blocked nose.

Asthma

Total duration of treatment:
7 MINUTES

Asthma is a chronic inflammatory disease of the respiratory tract. It is caused by hypersensitivity of the bronchial tubes and frequently connected with allergy problems. Infections of the bronchial tubes or the lungs are often a triggering factor. Asthma manifests as attacks of dyspnoea (shortness of breath) and wheezing, often at night, and is reversible spontaneously or with treatment. These attacks can be triggered by various factors such as pollen, humidity, pet dander (dead skin and hair), dust, dust mites, food products, strong emotions, cigarette smoke or exertion.

PRESSURE POINTS

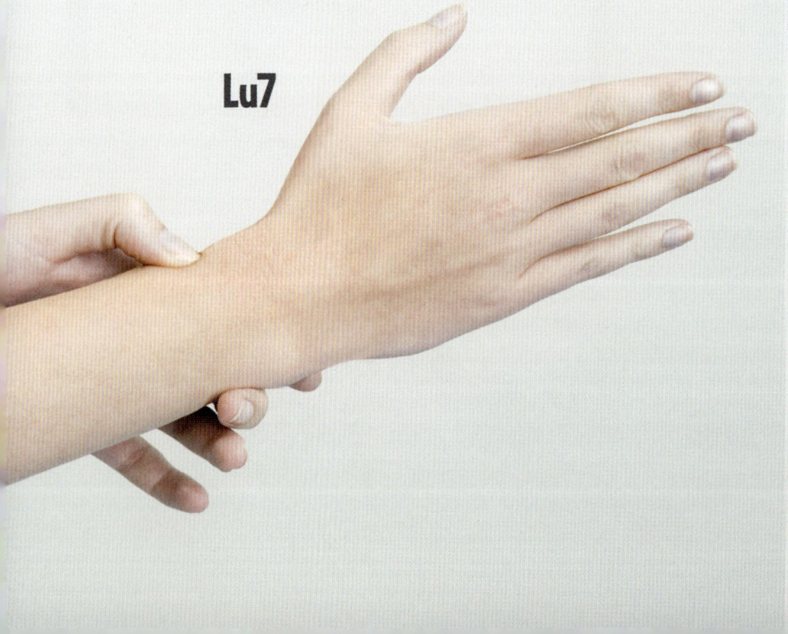

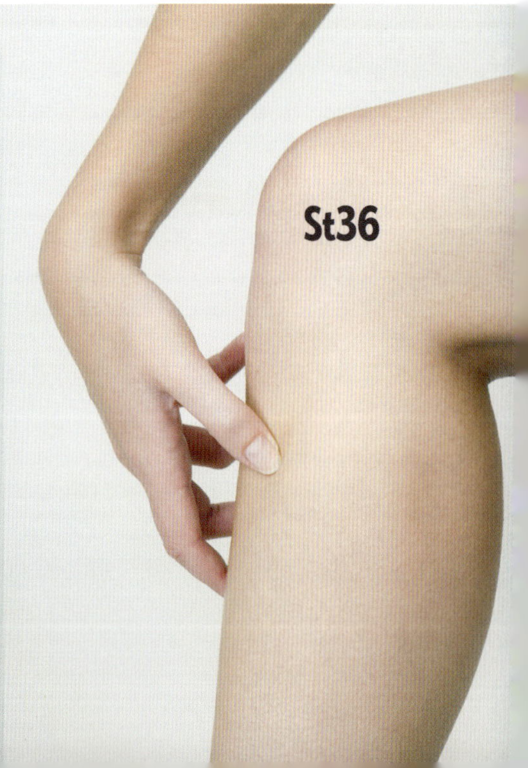

METHOD

Apply moderate pressure to each point with your thumb. Maintain this for 1 minute, then repeat the procedure on the opposite side. Do this a minimum of twice a day.

SOME EXTRA TIPS

- Mix 2 drops of **niaouli/paperbark essential oil**, 2 drops of **true lavender essential oil** and 3 drops of **sweet almond oil**. Massage this three times a day onto the solar plexus and the back.
- Avoid dairy products, fatty foods, foods that are too sweet or too salty, moistening foods, food that are too acidic (vinegar) and gluten. Instead, opt for nuts, sesame, almonds, chestnuts, mandarins, turnips, spinach ... Be careful with allergenic foods such as fish and seafood (prawns, crab, and so on).

IN TRADITIONAL CHINESE MEDICINE

The normal functioning of the lung depends on the support of other organs. The spleen gives the energy it creates to the lung, the liver's propulsion helps the lung lower qi and the kidney retains the qi sent downwards by the lung. External pathogens, food allergies, as well as emotional disturbances, damage the proper functioning of the lung and induce asthma attacks from an energy surplus or deficiency.

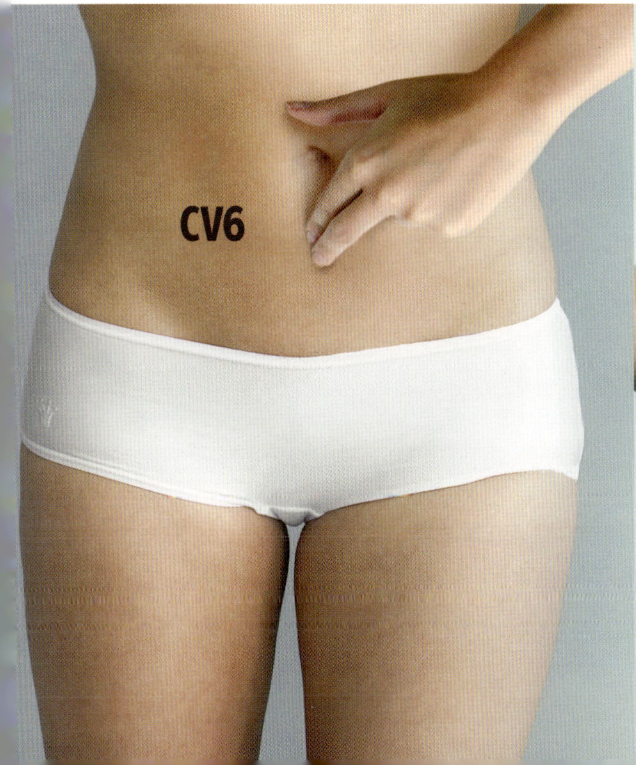

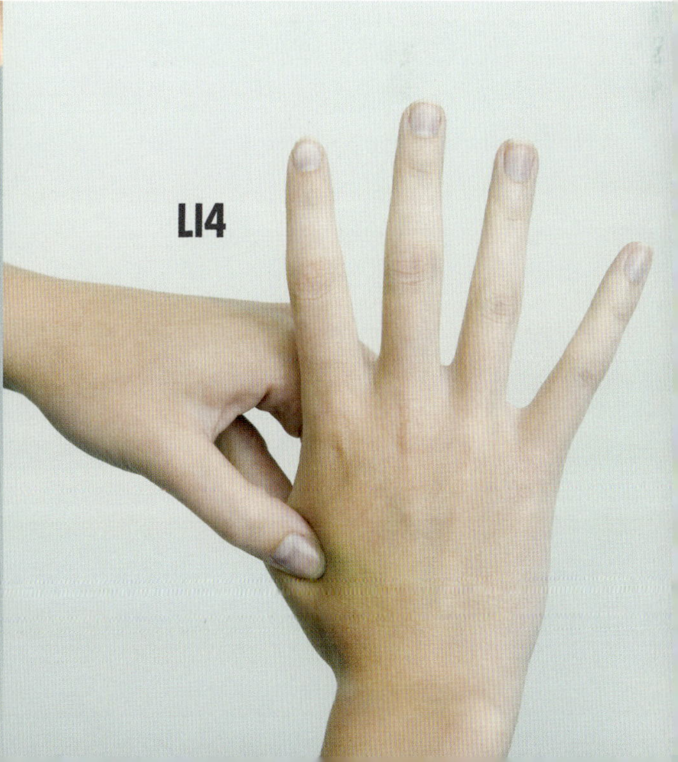

Ringing in the ears (tinnitus)

Total duration of treatment:
18 MINUTES

Tinnitus is defined as the perception of a sound inside the ear (buzzing, ringing, rumbling, whistling), which can be intermittent, continuous or pulsating, when no actual external noise is present. Various reasons can explain this auditory disorder, including repeated trauma (using a mobile telephone, exposure to high levels of sound), overwork and poor diet as well as sexual excesses and psycho-emotional disorders. Taking certain medications (antibiotics, aspirin, diuretics, antihypertensives) can also be the cause: don't hesitate to discuss this with your doctor.

METHOD

Apply moderate pressure to each point with your thumb. Maintain this for 2 minutes, then repeat the procedure on the opposite side.

SOME EXTRA TIPS

- To nourish the liver and the kidneys, which have a direct relationship with the ears, consume nuts, chestnuts and Euryale seeds (available from Chinese stores). Avoid cold and raw foods: cold narrows the Eustachian tubes, negatively affecting drainage of the inner ear. Also try eliminating gluten and dairy products, which increase the production of phlegm, hindering the correct distribution of energy.
- **Ginkgo biloba** (available from pharmacies) can help to stabilize tinnitus of the 'ringing' kind by increasing the circulation of the capillary blood.

VARIATION

You can also use the express point **TB6**: stimulate the point for 3 minutes.

PRESSURE POINTS

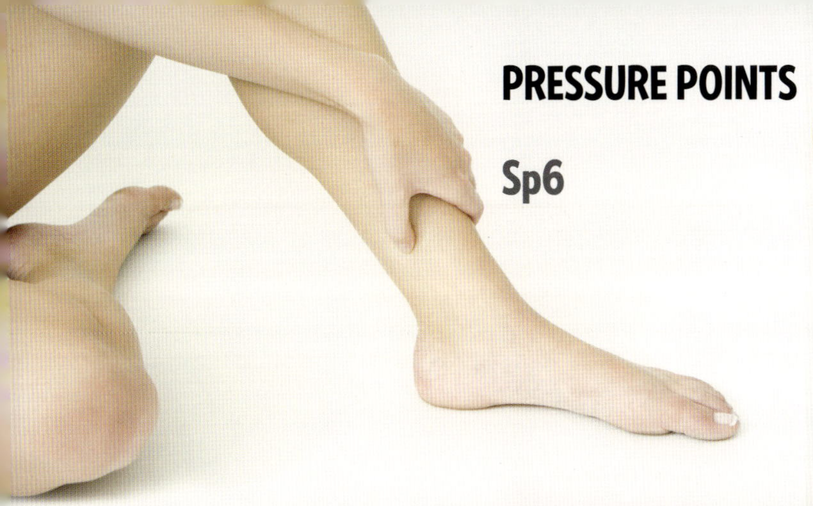

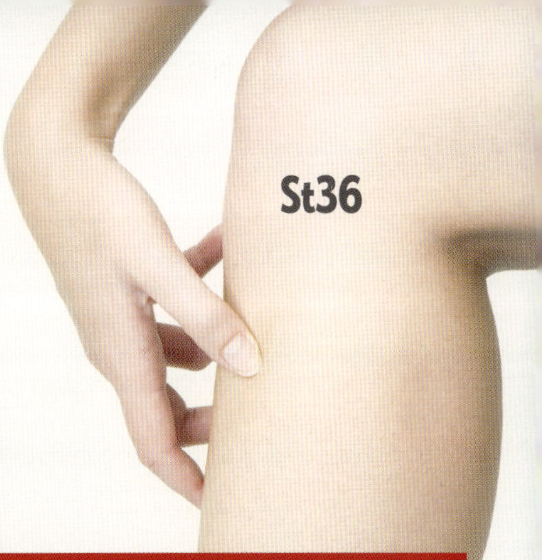

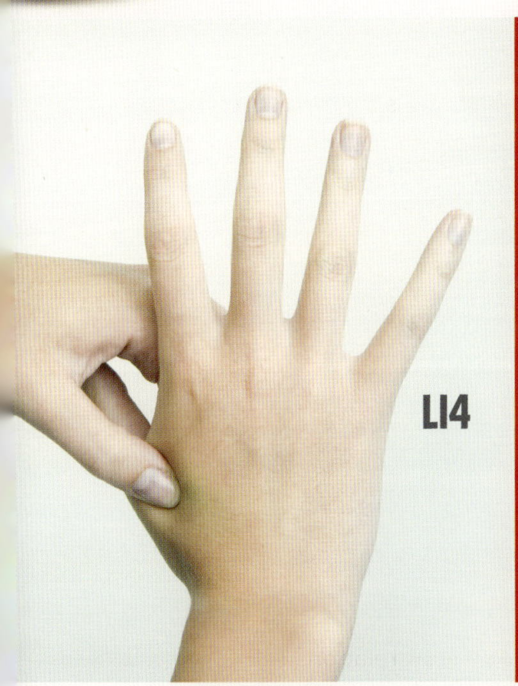

IN TRADITIONAL CHINESE MEDICINE

The ear is the energy orifice of the kidney. The kidney/bladder pair governs our hearing. Tinnitus is often associated with a progressive weakness of the kidneys, induced by stress, lack of sleep and excessive sexual activity. Negative emotions and emotional shocks are also often the cause: anger, frustration and resentment block the liver's energy. Over time, this stagnant energy is transformed into fire and rises towards the head, attacking the ears. This unhealthy lifestyle weakens the centre (spleen/stomach), resulting in a disturbance in the movement of energy and blood. Certain forms of tinnitus can also be set off by an accumulation of heat in the stomach, creating stagnation in the large intestine.

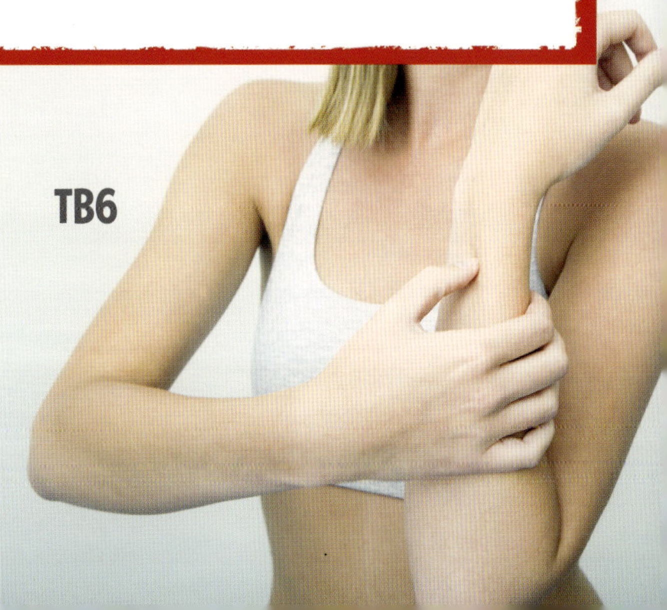

Sore throat

Total duration of treatment:
8 MINUTES

Most often benign, a sore throat can nonetheless prove to be very painful. In 85 per cent of cases, the cause is viral. Dry air and cold wind may also be factors. Sore throats can also be linked to prolonged efforts of the vocal cords and throat muscles: many singers, actors, public speakers – even teachers – suffer from this. The symptoms are generally a red throat that burns and irritates (typical signs of inflammation).
A sore throat is often the first symptom of a chill (cold, flu).

PRESSURE POINTS

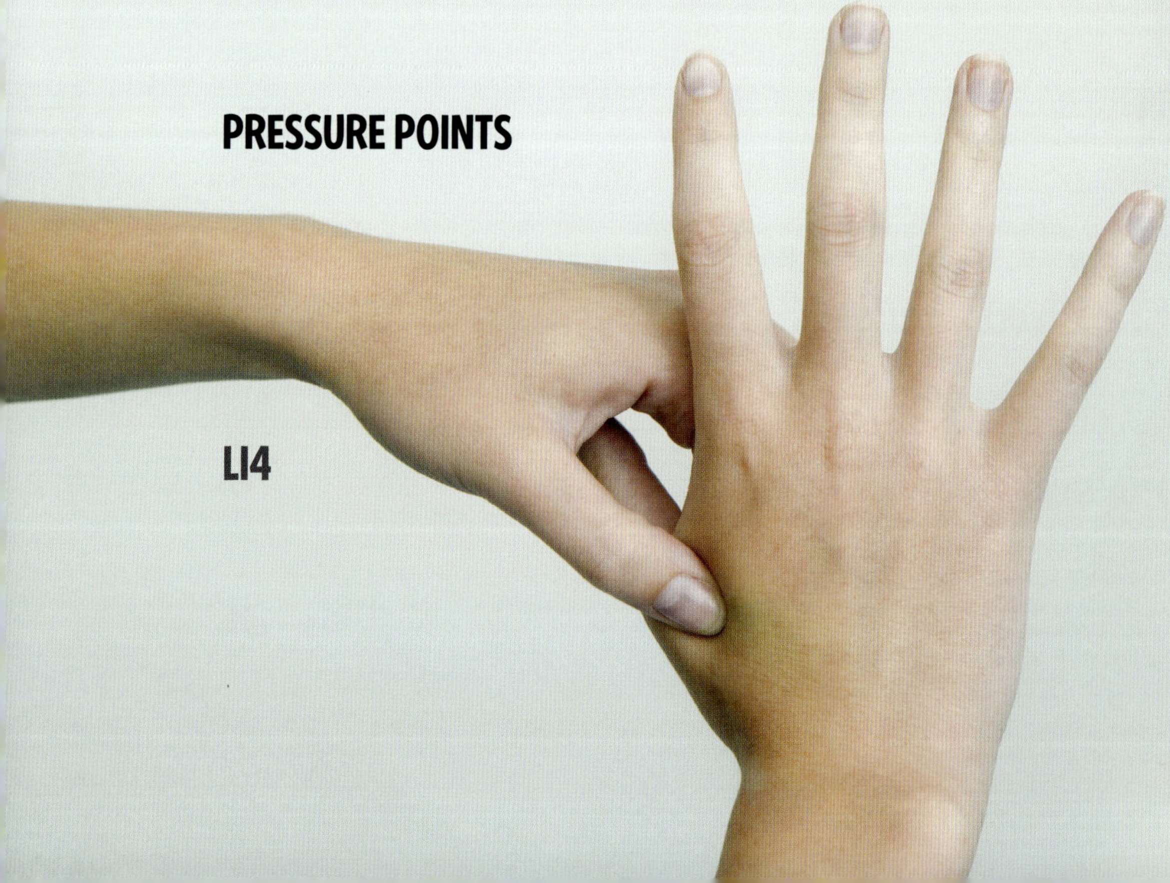

LI4

METHOD

- Apply moderate pressure to **LI4** and **TB6** with your thumb. Maintain this for 2 minutes, then repeat on the opposite side.
- Heat point **St36** with a moxa stick for 10 minutes.

SOME EXTRA TIPS

- Try fresh **pear tea** (**Xian Li Cha**). Make an infusion of 3g of tea and add a pear cut into slices. Stir and drink. This tea moistens the throat and produces body fluids.
- Try **colloidal silver** (available from health stores and pharmacies) – a natural antibiotic frequently used in the pre-antibiotic era, thanks to its antimicrobial, antibacterial and fungicidal properties. Take 1 tablespoon in the mornings on an empty stomach.

IN TRADITIONAL CHINESE MEDICINE

This imbalance is expressed in two ways – one cold and the other hot. The exogenous effect (coming from outside the body) is often generated by the perverse wind-heat energy, which weakens the lung, invades the body and attacks the throat. The endogenous imbalance (which comes from within the body) is often associated with deficiency of the kidney's liquid yin energy: the depleted liquids promote the agitation of fire, which, through the internal trajectory of the kidney meridian, affects the throat and creates an imbalance. It is important to protect the immune system, especially the lung and the kidney.

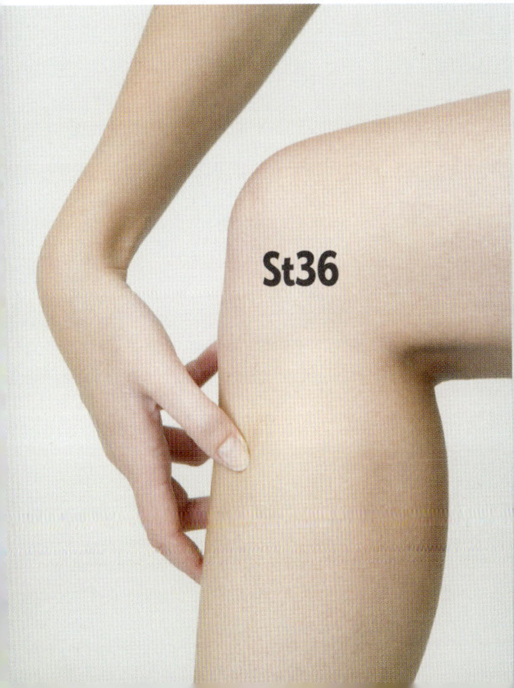

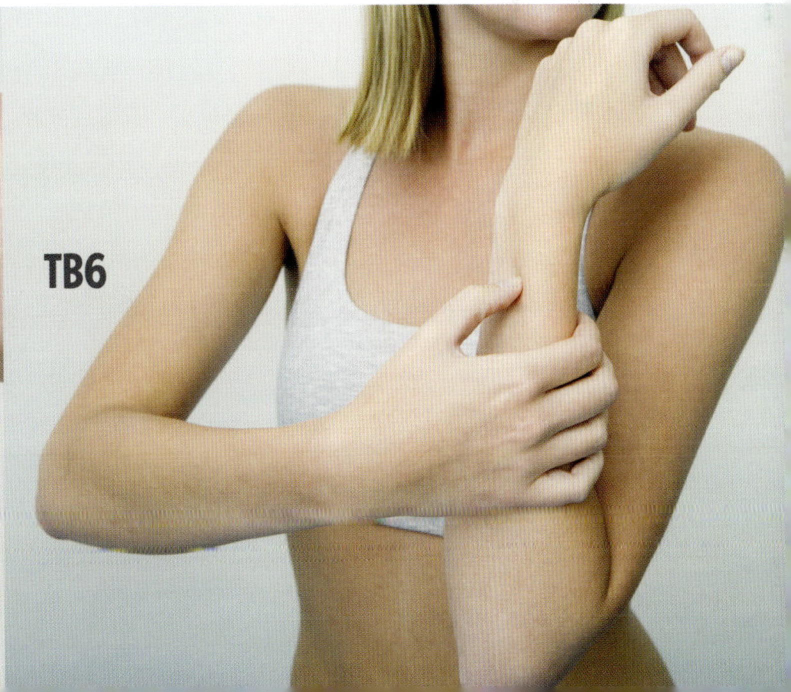

Loss of smell (anosmia)

Total duration of treatment:
14 MINUTES

Loss of smell is a distressing disorder. It can affect one nostril (partial anosmia) or both (complete anosmia). It is often a consequence of rhinitis, sinusitis or a viral infection.

METHOD

Apply moderate pressure to each point with your thumb. Maintain this for 2 minutes, then repeat the procedure on the opposite side.

THE PRINCIPAL POINT

Note that the principal point for regulating this disease is point **LI20**, the Chinese name for which is Ying Xiang, or 'welcome fragrance'.

PRESSURE POINTS

LI20

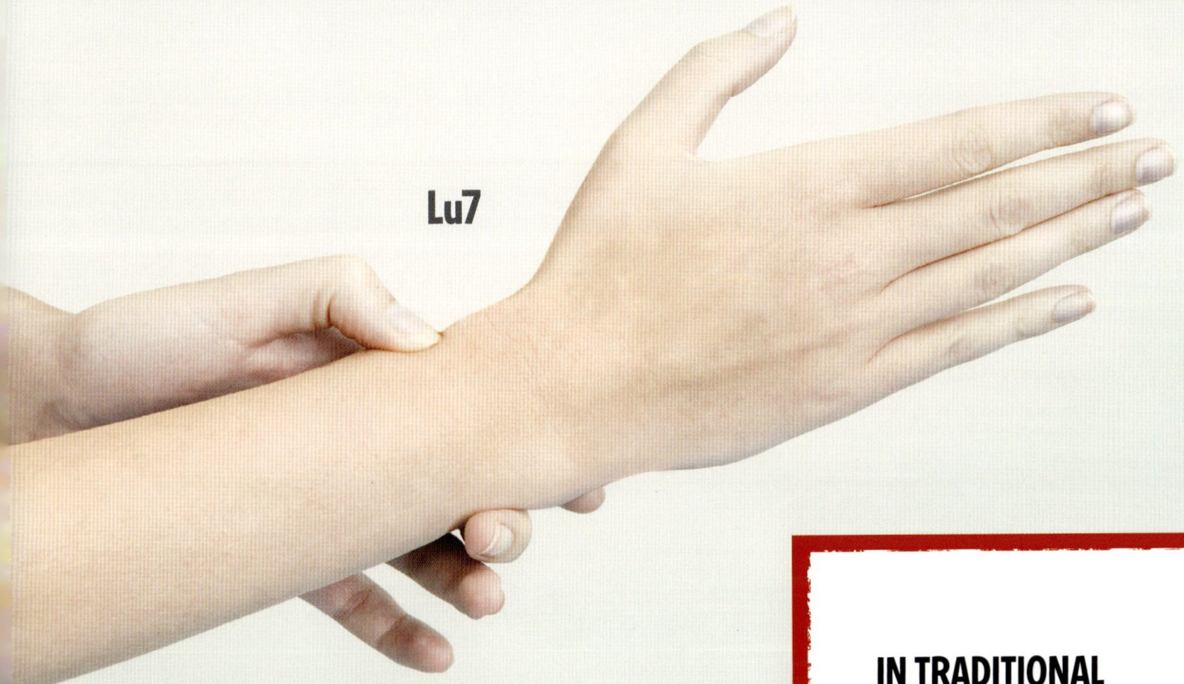

SOME EXTRA TIPS

- Mix 20 drops of **marjoram essential oil**, 10 drops of **rosemary essential oil** and 10 drops of **Himalayan spikenard essential oil** in a small bottle. Massage the solar plexus with 3 drops of this preparation in the mornings and at noon.
- For the right diet to adopt, see the advice for Rhinitis and Sinusitis (pages 91 and 95).
- Other traditional practices can be used as a complement, such as acupuncture, moxibustion, cupping therapy and foot reflexology.

IN TRADITIONAL CHINESE MEDICINE

The nose is the sense organ corresponding to the lung: it helps the lung's communication with the outside. The blockage of the lung's qi creates an obstruction in the nose and an inability to detect smells.

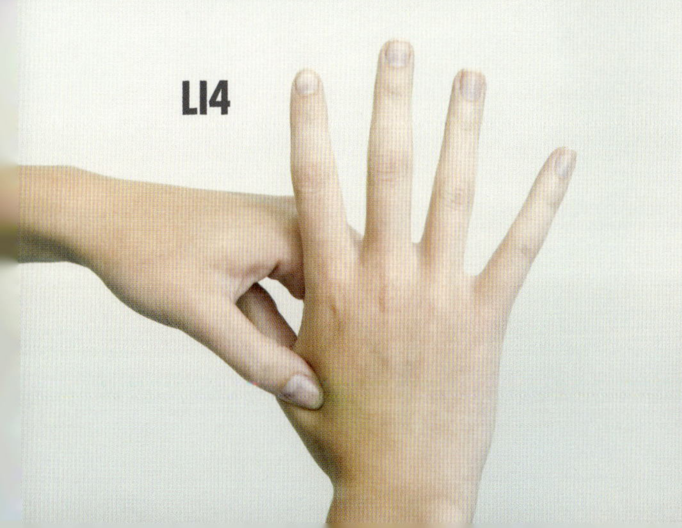

Acute rhinitis

Total duration of treatment:
10 MINUTES

Rhinitis is an acute (or chronic) inflammation of the mucous membrane in the nasal cavities due to infection, most frequently viral in origin. It translates into clear discharge with burning and a blocked-nose sensation. In the case of initial or secondary bacterial infection, the discharge becomes thick and yellow.

METHOD

Apply moderate pressure to each point with your thumb using tonification (in a clockwise direction). Maintain this for 1 minute, then repeat on the opposite side. Do this at least three times a day during an attack.

PRESSURE POINTS

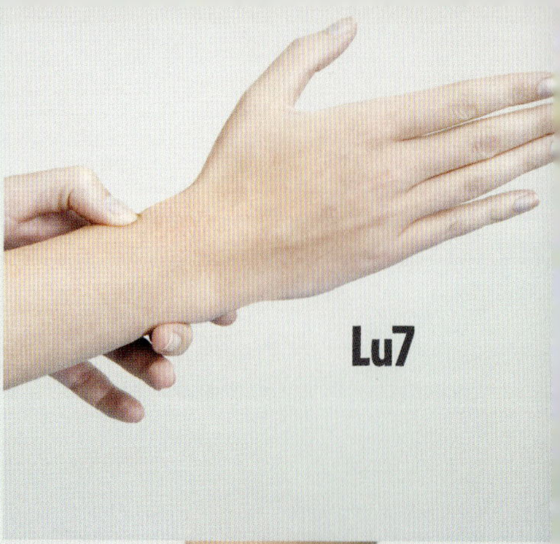

Lu7

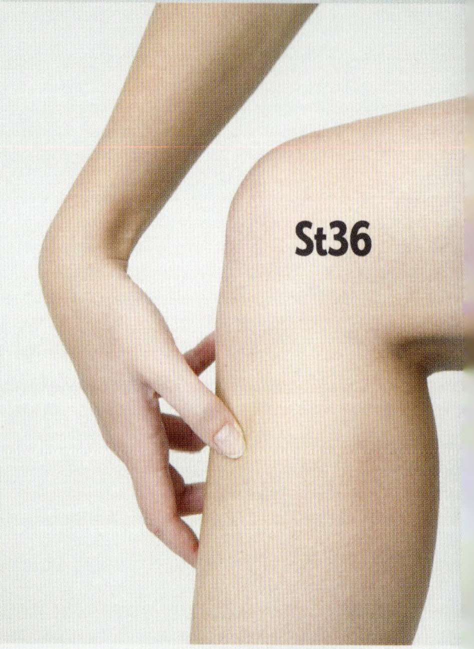

St36

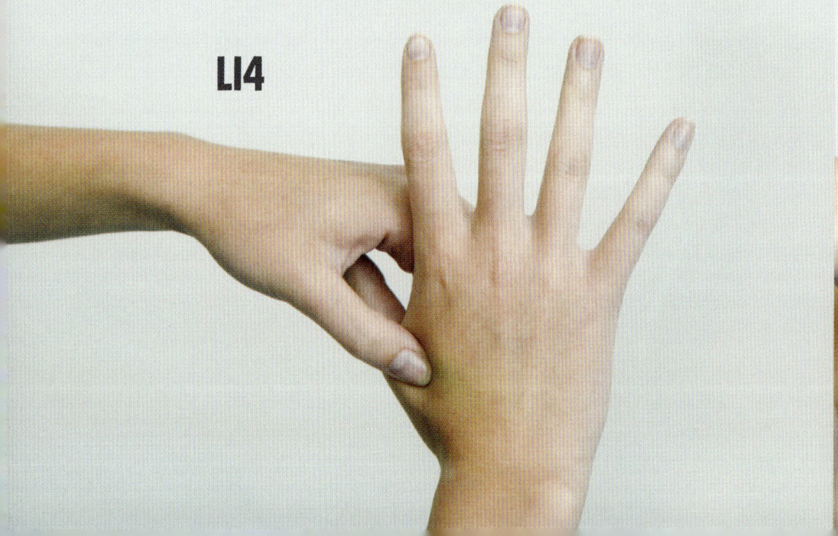

LI4

LI20

SOME EXTRA TIPS

- Mix 25 drops of **cineole rosemary essential oil**, 25 drops of **eucalyptus radiata essential oil** and 25 drops of **true lavender essential oil** in 30ml (1fl oz) of **sweet almond oil**. Administer 3 drops of this mixture into each nostril three times a day. You could also use **cineole rosemary essential oil** and **eucalyptus radiata essential oil** in diffusion. Not to be done on young children and pregnant women.
- Chew a small (1g) piece of **organic propolis** (available from health stores), as if chewing gum, for 1 to 2 hours, three times a day.
- Eliminate dairy products, which promote the production of phlegm and heat (see Sinusitis page 95).

IN TRADITIONAL CHINESE MEDICINE

The nose is the lung's orifice through which it communicates with the external world. The pathogens reach the lung through the nose. Wind, cold, humidity and heat promote stagnation of qi and of the blood in the nose and, consequently, in the lung. Weakness of qi in the spleen, the lung and the kidney, as well as environmental factors (such as variations in temperature, the level of humidity and atmospheric pollution) are also factors causing rhinitis.

Colds & flu

Total duration of treatment:
18 MINUTES

Colds and flu are viral infections of the upper respiratory tubes. They can be caused by various viruses.

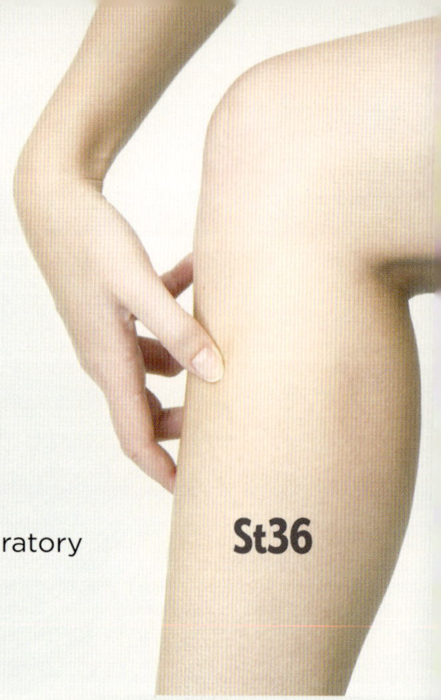

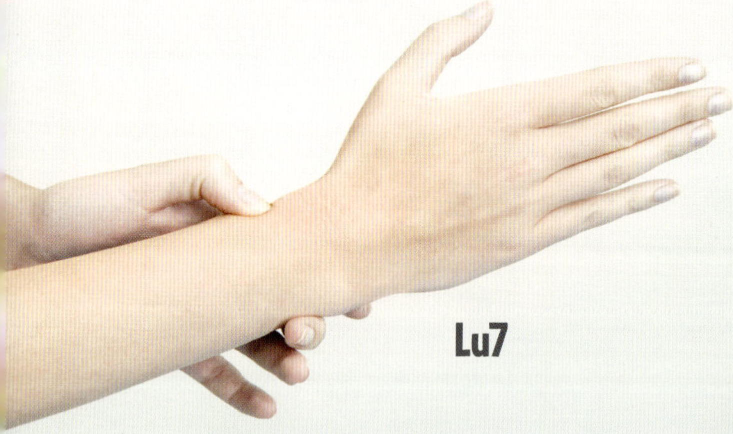

METHOD

Massage each point (except **St36**) using dispersion by applying moderate pressure with your thumb, maintaining this for 1 minute. Repeat the procedure on the opposite side. Then stimulate point **St36** with a moxa stick for 10 minutes.

PRESSURE POINTS

SOME EXTRA TIPS

- Take extract of **echinacea** (*Echinacea angustifolia* and/or *Echinacea purpurea*). For the correct dose, refer to the label.
- Avoid fatty foods, fish and meat, as well as gluten, which are all humidifying and allergenic. Instead, favour rice, legumes, sweet potatoes, yams and taro. The consumption of organic eggs is tolerated for supporting qi. Avoid alcohol and black tea – drink organic green or white tea.
- In a 5ml (⅙ fl oz) tinted glass bottle, mix 37 drops of **ravintsara essential oil**, 25 drops of **niaouli essential oil**, 25 drops of **thyme essential oil**, 25 drops of **peppermint essential oil** and 12 drops of **balsam fir essential oil**. Rub 2 to 3 drops of this mixture on the thorax and the lower back three times a day, as well as on a handkerchief to inhale several times a day.

IN TRADITIONAL CHINESE MEDICINE

Colds and flu correspond to invasions by external wind. They bring about a lowering of the body's resistance to pathogens, which manifest in the form of wind-cold, wind-heat, wind-heat-humidity or wind-heat-dryness. The lung controls the outside (the skin and body hair), and is connected to the throat and the external world through the nose. Wind blocks the upper layer, obstructing the movement of yang (heating) of the area, resulting in the aversion to cold. The fight between defensive energy and the pathogens creates a fever as well as a nutritional and defensive imbalance. It is important to nourish qi, blood and the immune system.

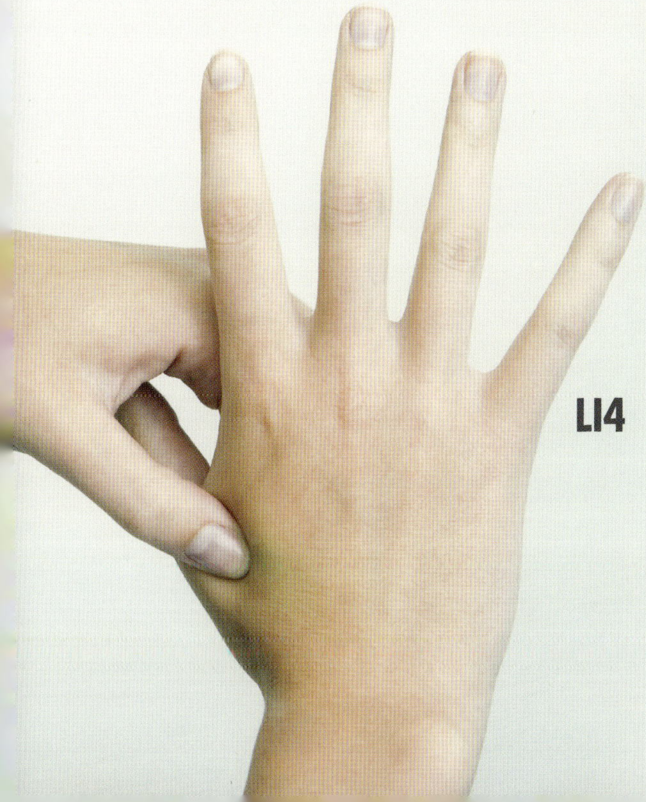

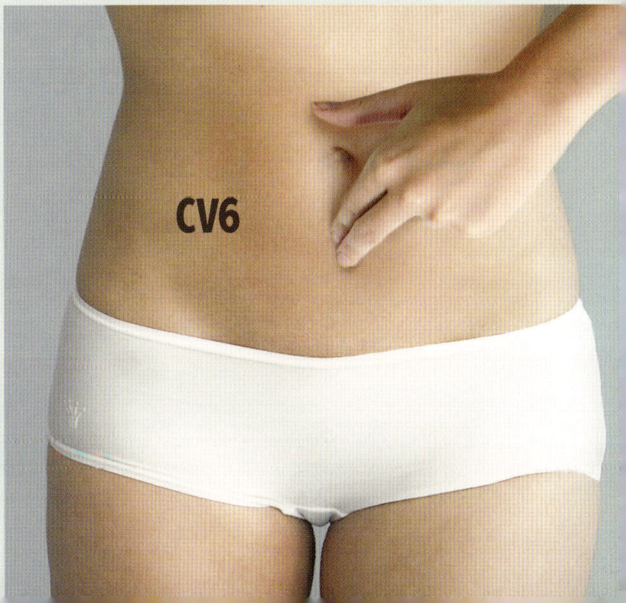

Sinusitis

Total duration of treatment:
12 MINUTES

Sinusitis is the inflammation of the sinuses – bone cavities filled with air – due to a bacterial or viral infection. It can be acute or chronic and, occasionally, there may also be an allergic factor. It manifests in the form of a discharge of pus from the nose, mild fever, headaches and, mostly, intense pain, the centre of which depends on the affected sinus. This attack often happens when there is an intestinal infection, playing an excretory role: the intestines are blocked and this is reflected in the sinuses.

PRESSURE POINTS

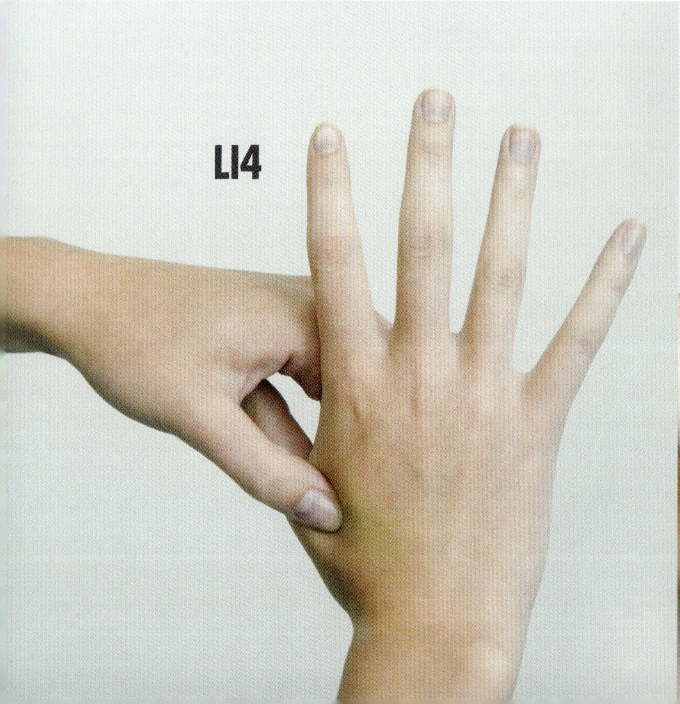

METHOD

Apply moderate pressure to each point with your thumb. Maintain this for 2 minutes, then repeat the procedure on the opposite side.

SINUSITIS OR RHINITIS?

With sinusitis, the nasal discharge is thick, sticky and yellow. With rhinitis, the nasal discharge is light and profuse.

SOME EXTRA TIPS

- Mix 5 drops of **niaouli essential oil** and 5 drops of **true lavender essential oil** in 1 tablespoon of **sweet almond oil**. Massage it in an anti-clockwise direction into the point **LI20** for 2 minutes.
- Cut out dairy products (milk, cheeses, yogurt), as they produce phlegm and heat, promoting the appearance of heat-humidity in the stomach and the spleen. This heat-humidity can rise up to the sinuses along the stomach meridian.

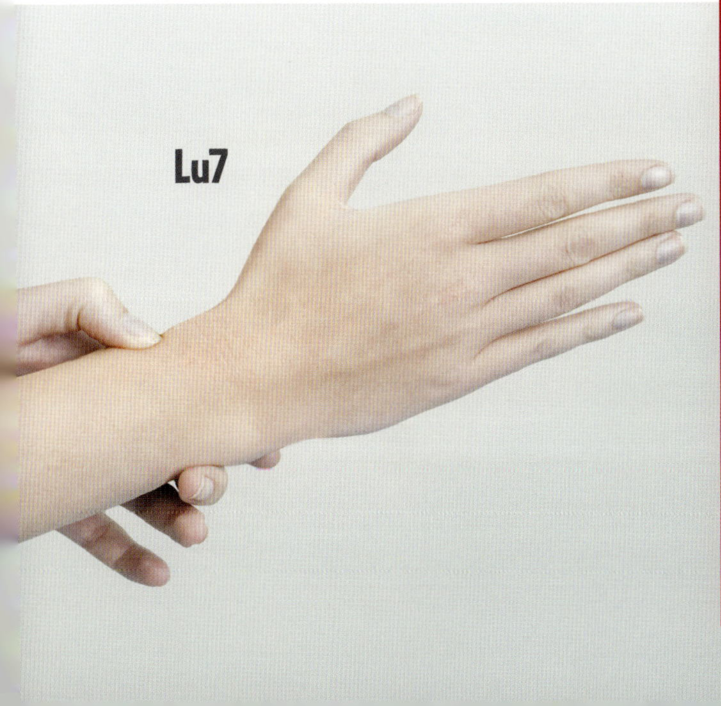

IN TRADITIONAL CHINESE MEDICINE

The lung continuously communicates with the external world via the nose. Sinusitis is due to wind, wind-heat or wind-cold pathogens, which disturb the spreading and descent of the lung's qi into the bone cavities. This causes a stagnation of fluids in the nose and the sinuses. This prolonged stagnation of fluids, produced by phlegm and heat, manifests as yellow and purulent nasal discharge. If the pathogens are not totally destroyed, heat persists in the nose, causing rhinorrhoea disorders, which turn into chronic sinusitis.

Abdominal pain

Total duration of treatment:
18 MINUTES

Abdominal pains are very common and can be attributed to many factors, whether digestive, gynaecological or psychosomatic in nature.

METHOD

- Apply moderate pressure to **TB6** and **P6** with your thumb. Maintain this for 2 minutes, then repeat the procedure on the opposite side.
- Heat point **St36** with a moxa stick for 10 minutes.

PRESSURE POINTS

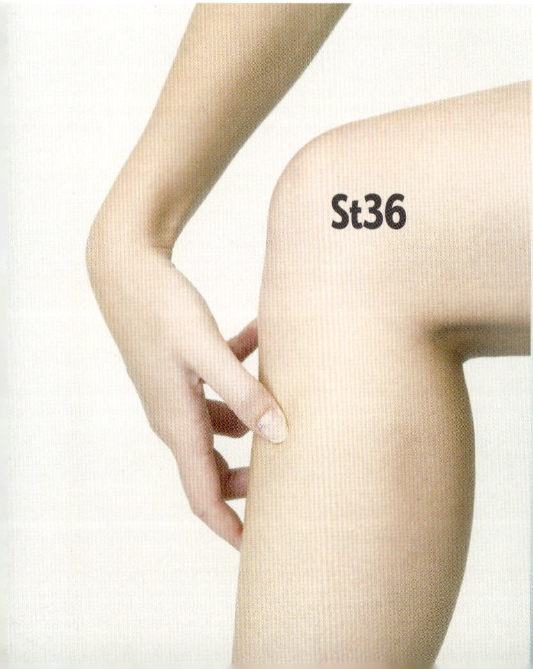

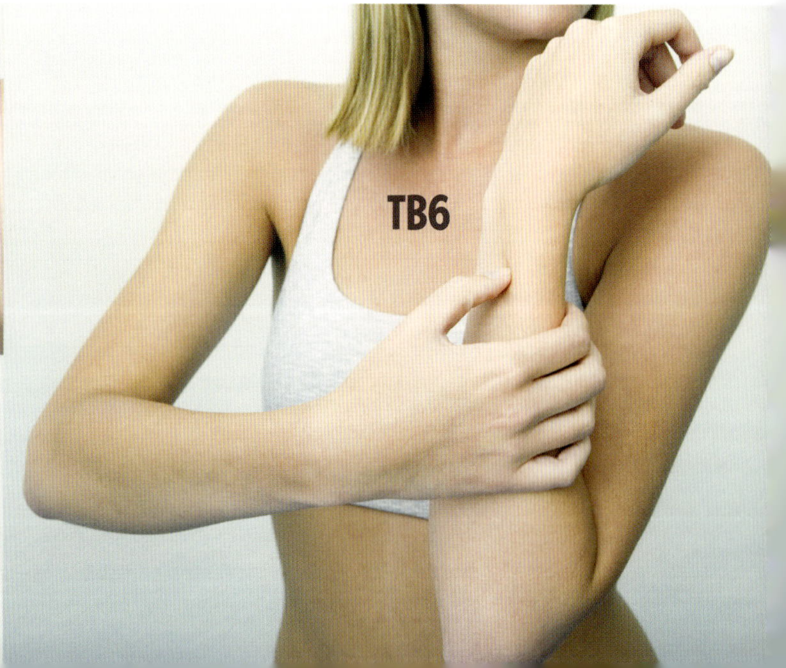

SOME EXTRA TIPS

- In a tinted glass bottle with a dropper, mix 15ml (½fl oz) of **hazelnut vegetable oil**, 50 drops of **tarragon essential oil**, 50 drops of **peppermint essential oil**, 25 drops of **roman chamomile essential oil**, 25 drops of **sweet fennel essential oil**, and 25 drops of **coriander essential oil**. Massage 8 drops of this preparation onto your stomach, two to five times a day.
- Eliminate gluten and dairy products from your diet. Check food labels for monosodium glutamate (E621) and aspartame (E951).

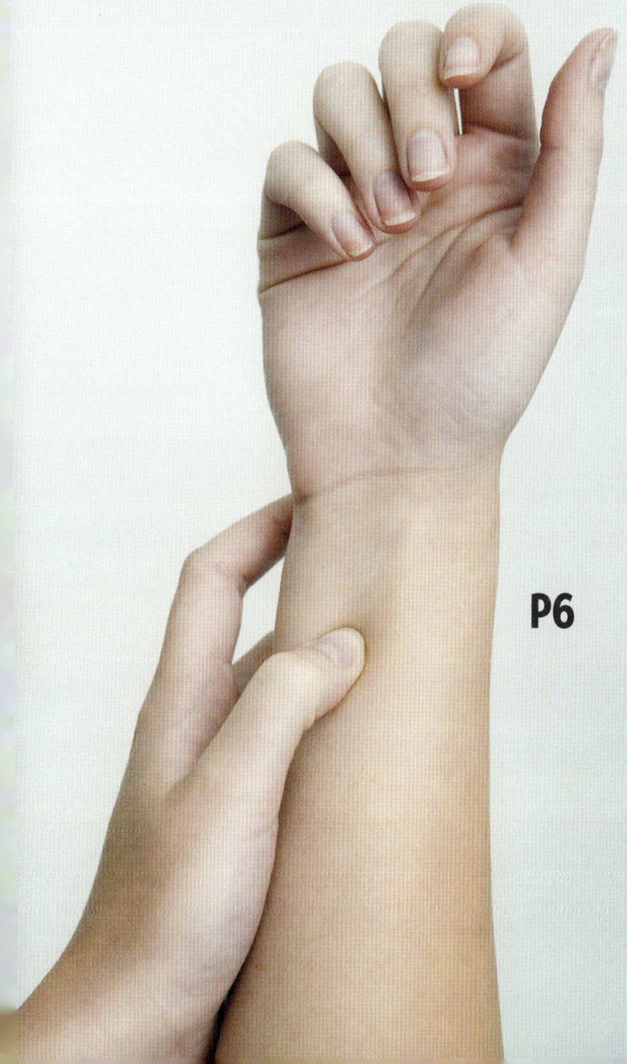

IN TRADITIONAL CHINESE MEDICINE

Poor diet (an excess of raw or cold foods) allows the penetration of cold into the abdomen, impairing yang and disturbing the spleen's function of transport and transformation. The stagnant cold causes contraction and this leads to abdominal pain. Excessive fatty, fried and spicy foods impede the digestive function of the stomach and the intestines. The slowing down of the spleen and/or insufficient yang-qi disturbs the transport/transformation activity, creates an accumulation of cold-humidity and results in abdominal pain.

Pain in the ribs

Total duration of treatment:
6 MINUTES

Pain in the flanks (the upper lateral abdominal area) and the ribs can be subjective or objective. It may be due to intercostal neuralgia, or be a psychosomatic manifestation of conditions such as depression or hyperventilation.

METHOD

- Apply strong pressure with your thumb to the point **TB6** located on the opposite side of the pain (so, on the left side if you feel pain on the right, and vice versa). Maintain this for 2 minutes.
- Also apply strong pressure with your thumb to point **UB40**, on both sides. Maintain this for 2 minutes on each side.

PRESSURE POINTS

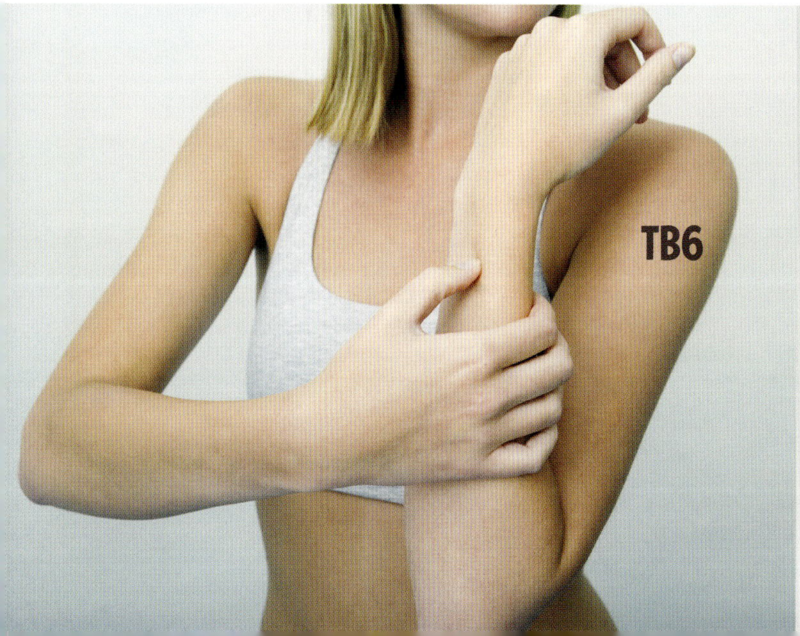

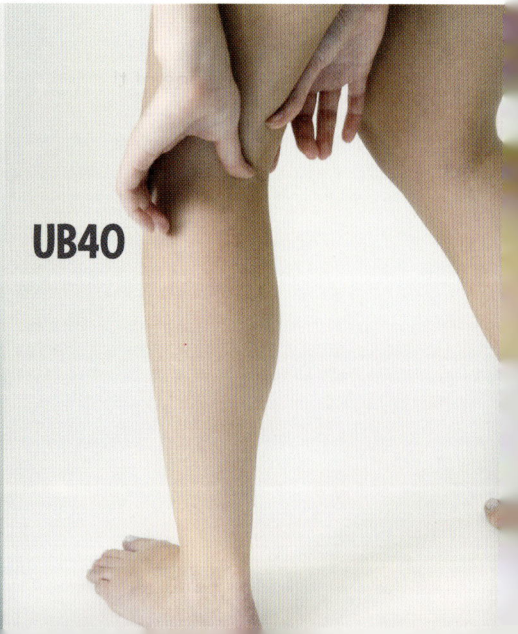

AN EXTRA TIP

In a 30ml (1fl oz) tinted glass bottle with a dropper, mix 5ml (⅙ fl oz) of **macadamia vegetable oil**, 5ml of **copaiba balsam**, 175 drops of **wintergreen essential oil**, 125 drops of **lemon eucalyptus essential oil**, 125 drops of **rosemary essential oil** and 75 drops of **copaiba essential oil**. Massage 10 drops of this preparation into the painful area two to five times a day.

IN TRADITIONAL CHINESE MEDICINE

The liver nourishes the flanks. Stress and depression can bring about a blockage of the liver's qi, causing pain. A chronic disease, heavy menstrual bleeding or stress can lead to an emptying of qi and blood, which then becomes insufficient to nourish the liver. Mental hyperactivity, rumination and worries, sexual excess, ageing and long-term illnesses also weaken the liver's yin, which can transform into excessive pressure on the liver, a fire in the liver (all stagnation is transformed into fire) and stasis of the liver's blood. A diet that is spicy, hot and sugary, with alcohol, dairy products and fried foods, attacks the spleen and the stomach, the liver and the gall bladder, and produces stagnant heat-humidity, which can also induce pain.

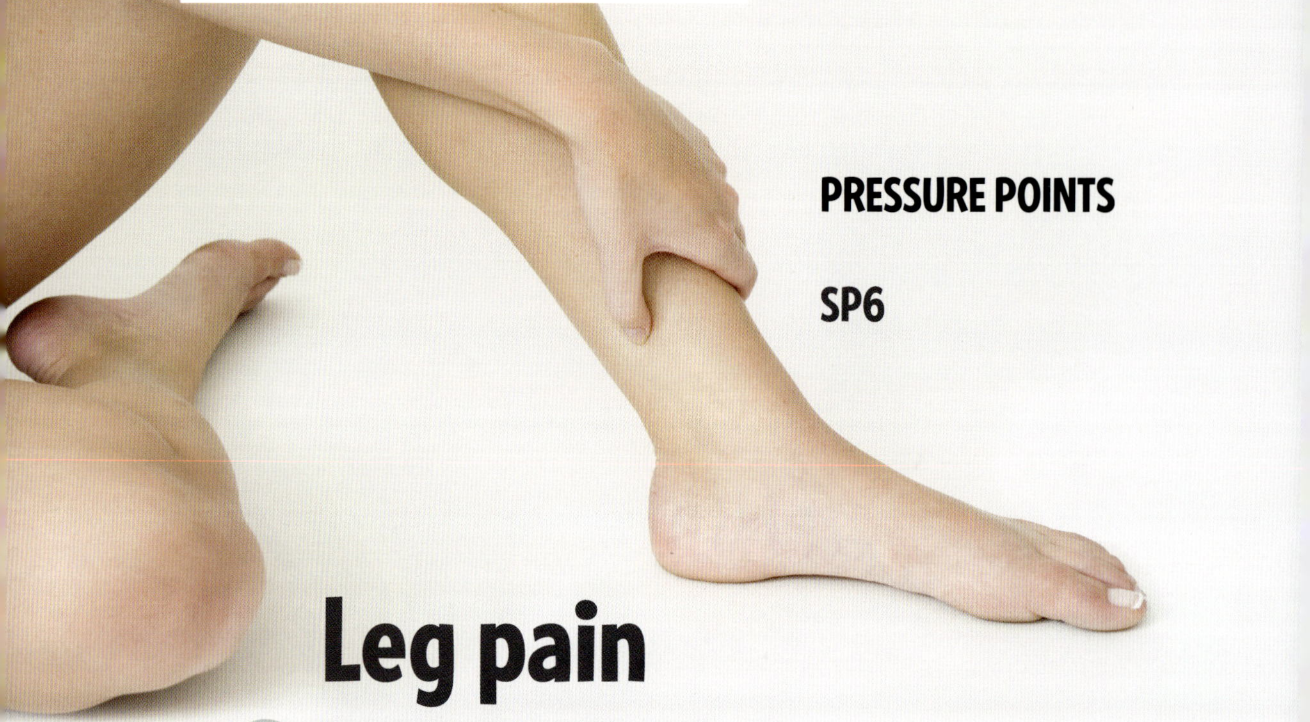

PRESSURE POINTS

Leg pain

Total duration of treatment:
12 MINUTES

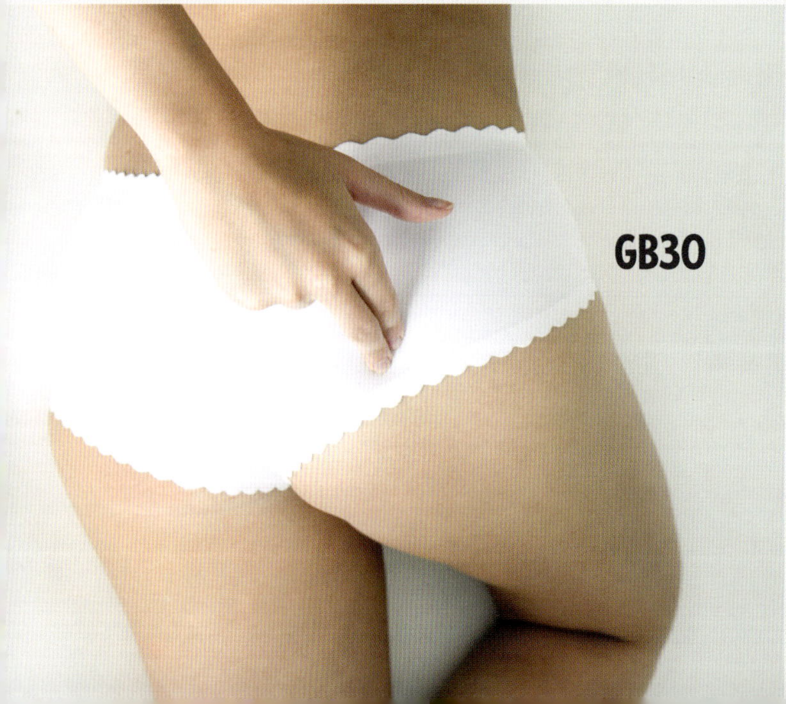

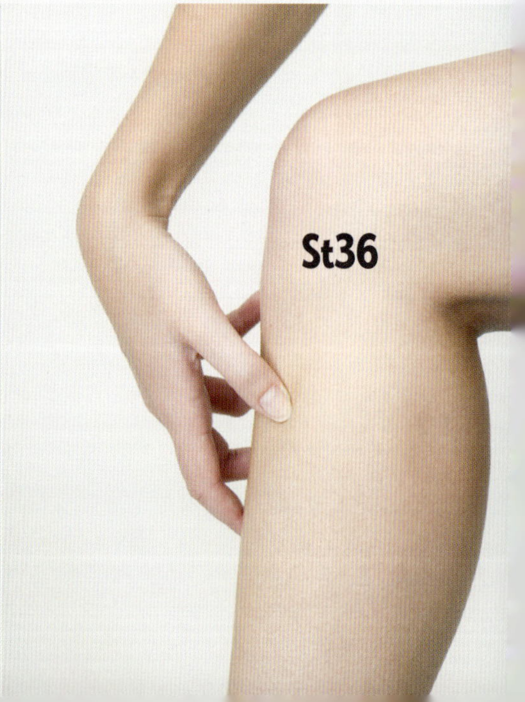

Leg pain is often attributed to a paralysis, damage in the common peroneal nerve, neuralgia, sciatica (see also page 122), rheumatic fever or a muscular sprain.

METHOD

Apply moderate pressure to each point with your thumb. Maintain this for 2 minutes, then repeat on the opposite side.

AN EXTRA TIP

In a tinted glass bottle, mix 15ml (½ fl oz) of **hypericum plant oil**, 50 drops of **helichrysum essential oil**, 50 drops of **thyme essential oil**, 50 drops of **ylang-ylang essential oil**, 50 drops of **wintergreen essential oil**, 25 drops of **chamomile essential oil**, 25 drops of **peppermint essential oil**, and 25 drops of **bay laurel essential oil**. Apply 5 drops on the painful area five times a day.

IN TRADITIONAL CHINESE MEDICINE

Stress, chronic disease, a weak constitution, sexual excess and ageing can lead to exhaustion of the kidney's Jing-essence, which can bring about its depletion and a weakness in qi and the blood. The legs are not properly nourished, resulting in pain and weakness. Physical trauma or stress can cause qi and blood to stagnate in the meridians, leading to stabbing pains in the legs. The depletion of qi and blood also causes pain in the legs due to the undernourishment of the meridians. The humidity-heat and the accumulation of phlegm-humidity (due to a high-fat diet, an excess of sugar, alcohol and dairy products) stagnate at the bottom of the body, blocking free movement in the meridians and inducing pain.

Hand pain

Total duration of treatment:
12 MINUTES

This may be located in the palm of one hand or both, and may be accompanied by swelling or numbing of the palm, a sensation of cold or heat, red blotches or, conversely, pallor, as well as pain in the finger joints. In the West, these imbalances are seen in conditions such as rheumatoid polyarthritis, gout, rheumatoid arthritis, carpal arthritis and carpal tunnel syndrome.

PRESSURE POINTS

Lu7

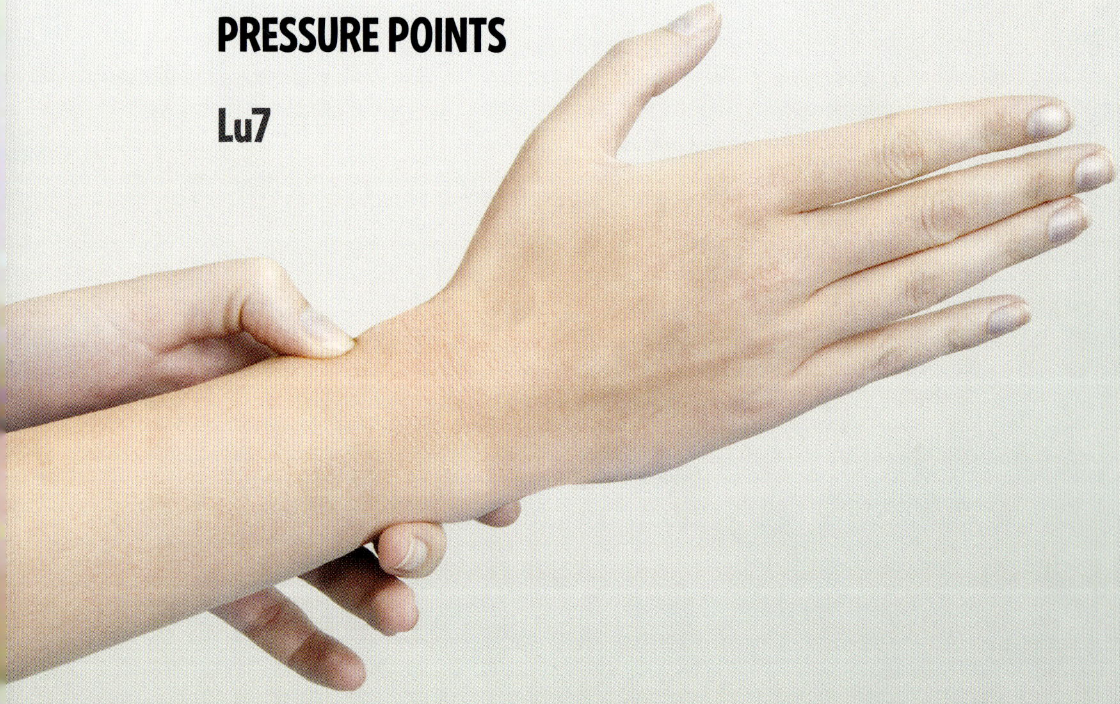

P6

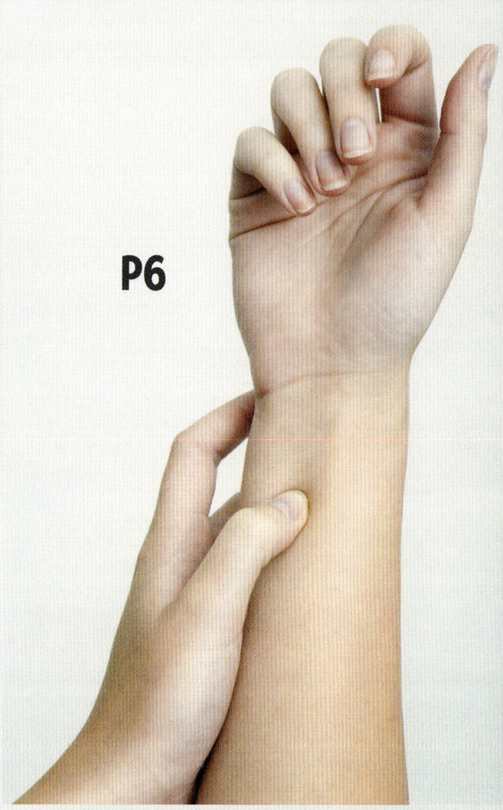

METHOD

Apply moderate pressure to each point with your thumb. Maintain this for 2 minutes, then repeat the procedure on the opposite side.

AN EXTRA TIP

Massage 10 drops of the **essential oil preparation** on page 97 into the painful area, two to five times a day.

VARIATION

You can also apply a moxa stick on the painful area (if it isn't hot), until it reddens (around 10 to 15 minutes).

IN TRADITIONAL CHINESE MEDICINE

Cold–humidity or humidity-heat invades the palm and blocks the circulation of qi and blood in the meridians as well as the nutrition of the tendons and the flesh, leading to pain. In addition, anger, frustrations and resentment lead to liver blockage. This results in a slowing down of qi and blood, which, over time, generates a stasis of the blood and an emptying of yang-qi in the meridians and the finger joints. An excess of spicy foods, alcohol, dairy products and sugar forms humidity-heat, which transforms into toxic fire and creates pain.

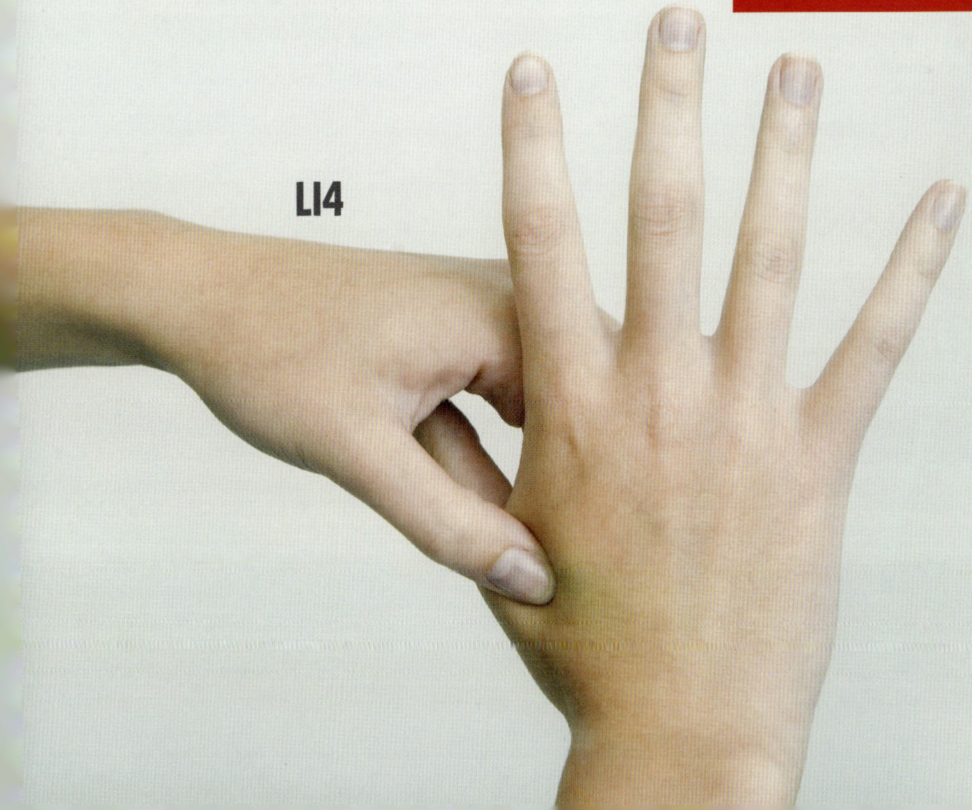

Breast pain

Total duration of treatment:
12 MINUTES

Pain in the breasts occurs frequently along with menstrual discomfort (irregular and/or painful periods) or when breastfeeding (congestion, blocked milk ducts, mastitis).

CAUTION!

Never apply moxibustion, and do not apply formulas based on essential oils on your breast. Consult your doctor if the discomfort persists.

METHOD

Apply moderate pressure to each point with your thumb. Maintain this for 2 minutes, then repeat the procedure on the opposite side.

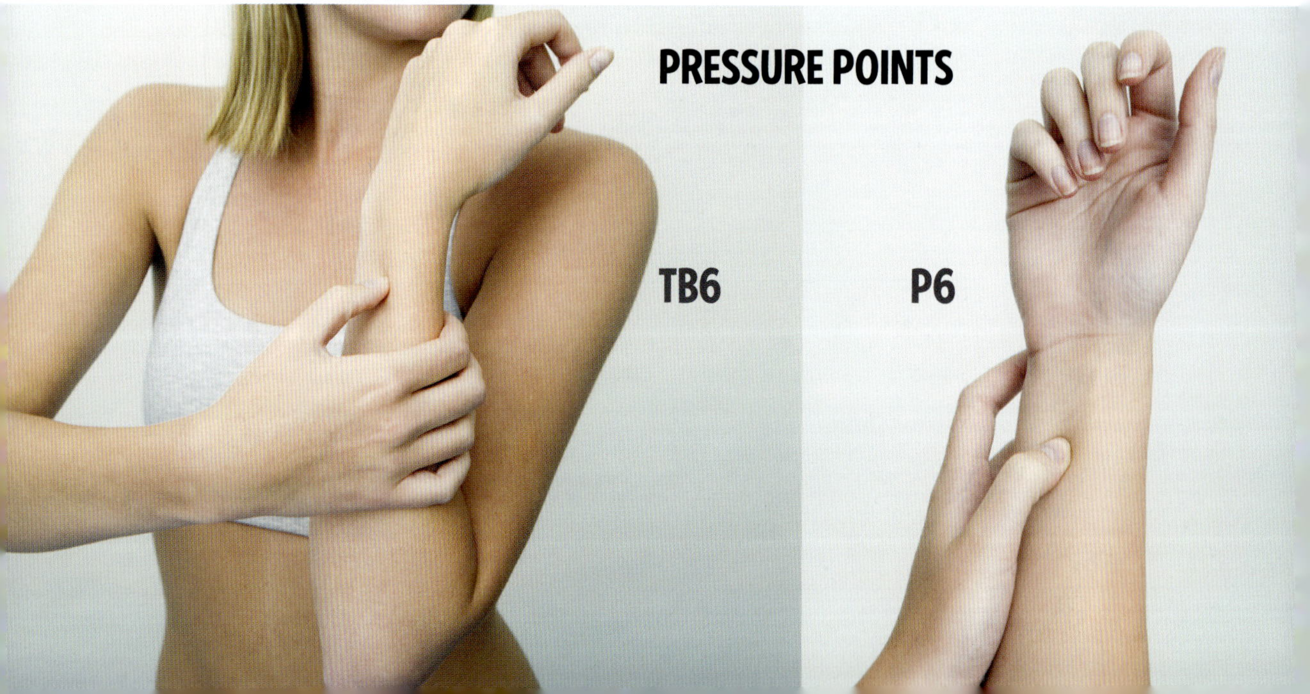

IN TRADITIONAL CHINESE MEDICINE

Affective and emotional factors are very important. The liver is in charge of the nipples: its energy route enters from the diaphragm, the flank area and the chest, and reaches the nipples. Frustration, anger or stress causes an imbalance in the liver's regulatory functions, leading to a blockage of qi and blood. This blockage, via the meridians that go along the breast, induces pain and distension in the area. Excess milk production can lead to a permanent fullness of the breast and disturbs the free movement of qi and blood. Diet also plays a role: an excess of raw and cold foods damages the yang-qi and the spleen/stomach and induces an accumulation of cold and humidity. The consumption of spicy and fatty foods leads to a stagnation of qi, blood and heat-humidity, and creates pain.

Back pain (generalized)

Total duration of treatment:
8 MINUTES

Many people complain of back pain – and there are a number of possible reasons for this! Among the most common, sedentariness comes to mind. The spine is designed for mobility; if it doesn't move sufficiently, or moves badly, it can result in pain. Other possible factors include repetitive actions, excess weight, an unbalanced diet (which promotes inflammation), congenital diseases (scoliosis), and the like.

METHOD

Apply moderate pressure to each point with your thumb. Maintain this for 2 minutes, then repeat the procedure on the opposite side.

PRESSURE POINTS

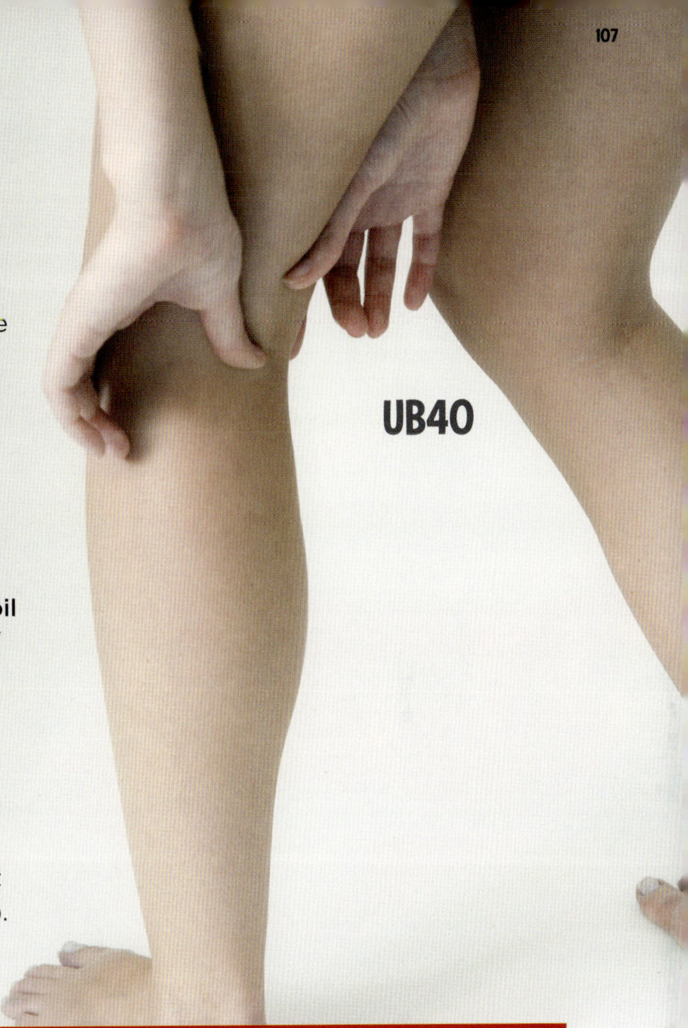

SOME EXTRA TIPS

- Pay attention to the quality of your bed. It should neither be too hard nor too soft; otherwise, it can encourage qi and blood to stagnate in the meridians running along the back, and this induces generalized back pain.
- In a tinted glass bottle with a dropper, mix 15ml (½ fl oz) of **calophyllum vegetable oil**, 150 drops of **helichrysum essential oil**, 50 drops of **wintergreen essential oil** and 50 drops of **pistacia lentiscus/ mastic pistachio essential oil**. Apply 5 drops five times a day on the painful area.

VARIATION

You can also use moxa sticks to heat the painful area (if the area isn't hot). Do this for 10–15 minutes.

IN TRADITIONAL CHINESE MEDICINE

Lack of physical exercise leads to a weakening of the tendons, muscles and joints. As a result, this slows down the free movement of qi and blood, leading to stagnation, and therefore pain. Stress and a weak constitution, heavy menstrual periods and chronic diseases also promote a depletion of qi, blood, yin and yang, developing an area of emptiness. The warming of the meridians, as well as the nutrition of the body, the muscles and the tendons, is less fluid and results in generalized back pain. Physical trauma (falls, accidents, wounds) can also damage the muscles, tendons and meridians, causing qi and blood to stagnate. Emotional troubles may also explain the pain: they block the liver's qi, preventing the free movement of qi throughout the body. Finally, external climate attacks (wind, cold, heat or humidity) can also block the meridians, leading to stagnation of qi and blood, and, consequently, to pain.

Knee pain

Total duration of treatment:
8 MINUTES

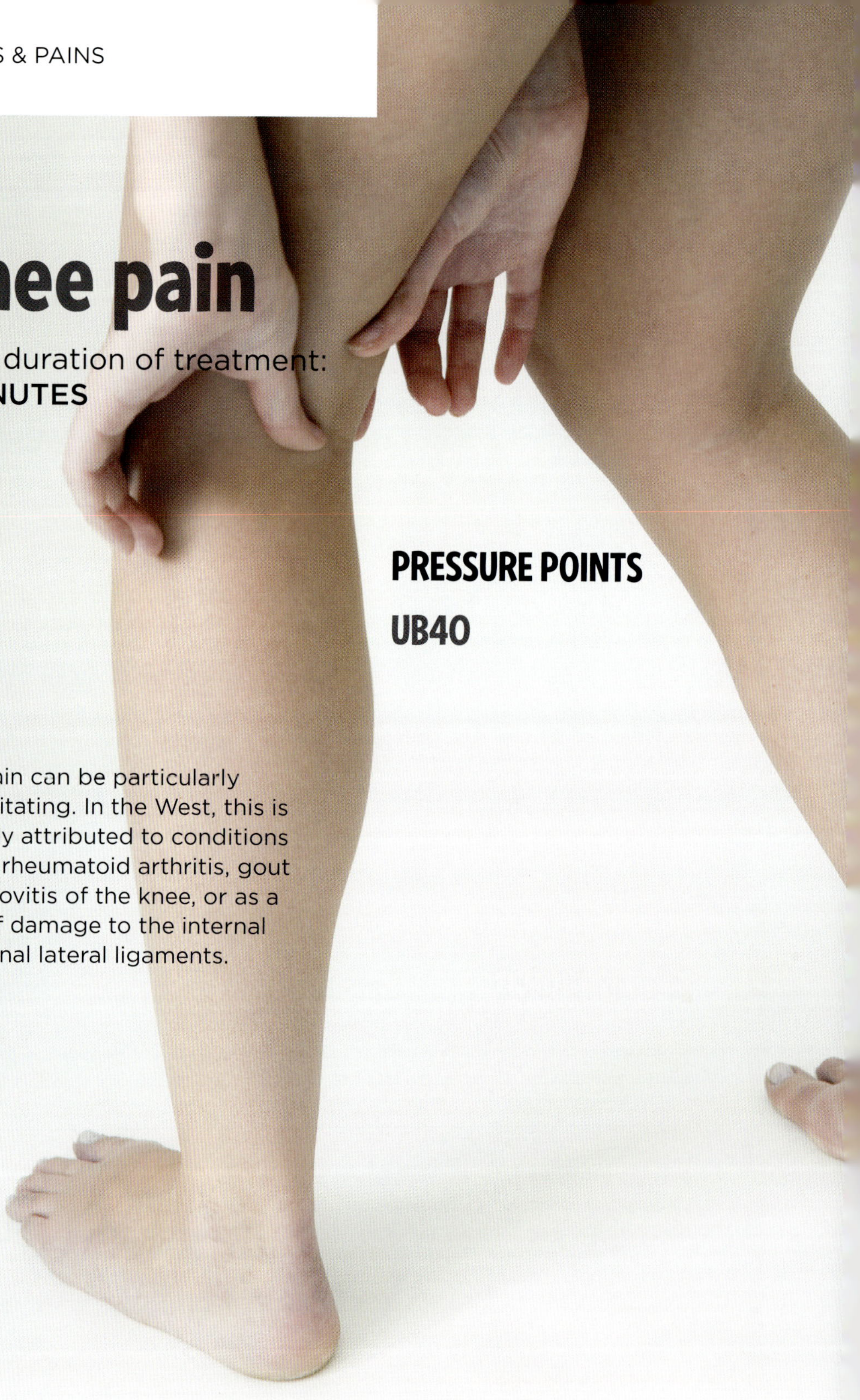

PRESSURE POINTS

UB40

Knee pain can be particularly incapacitating. In the West, this is generally attributed to conditions such as rheumatoid arthritis, gout and synovitis of the knee, or as a result of damage to the internal or external lateral ligaments.

METHOD

Apply moderate pressure to each point with your thumb. Maintain this for 2 minutes, then repeat on the opposite side.

VARIATION

You can also heat the painful area (if the area isn't hot) using moxa sticks for 10–15 minutes.

AN EXTRA TIP

Apply 10 drops of the **essential oil preparation** on page 97 onto the painful area, two to five times a day.

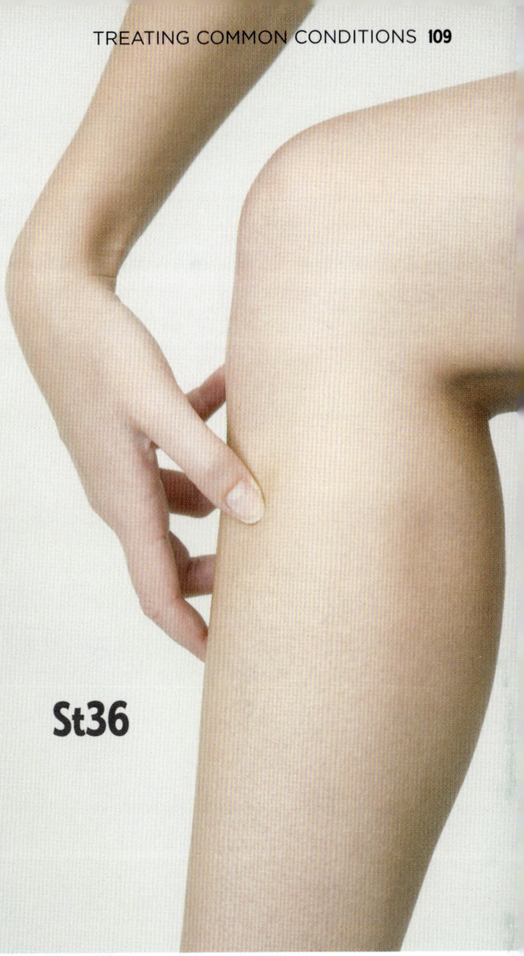

IN TRADITIONAL CHINESE MEDICINE

Physical trauma (bumps, falls) causes a blockage of qi and blood, leading to stagnation of the meridians and pain and swelling in the knees. Stress, ageing and chronic diseases also deplete qi and blood: the knees are therefore not properly nourished, resulting in pain. Fatigue, a weak constitution or sexual excesses can also lead to the depletion of qi, blood and depletion of the liver (which governs the tendons) and depletion of the kidney (which governs the cartilages and bones). Climate factors (wind, cold, heat and humidity) can also slow down the general circulation of qi and blood and limit joint mobility. An unbalanced diet (too much fat and sugar), or excess of dairy products and alcohol, causes damage to the spleen and the stomach by creating humidity and heat, which descend to block the meridians and cause knee pain.

Wrist pain

Total duration of treatment:
12 MINUTES

Wrist pain is generally attributed to tendinitis, neuralgia or tenosynovitis (inflammation of the tendon and its synovial sheath). It could also be a symptom of rheumatism or rheumatoid polyarthritis.

METHOD

Apply moderate pressure to each point with your thumb. Maintain this for 2 minutes, then repeat the procedure on the opposite side.

VARIATION

You can also heat the painful area (if the area isn't hot) using moxa sticks for 10–15 minutes.

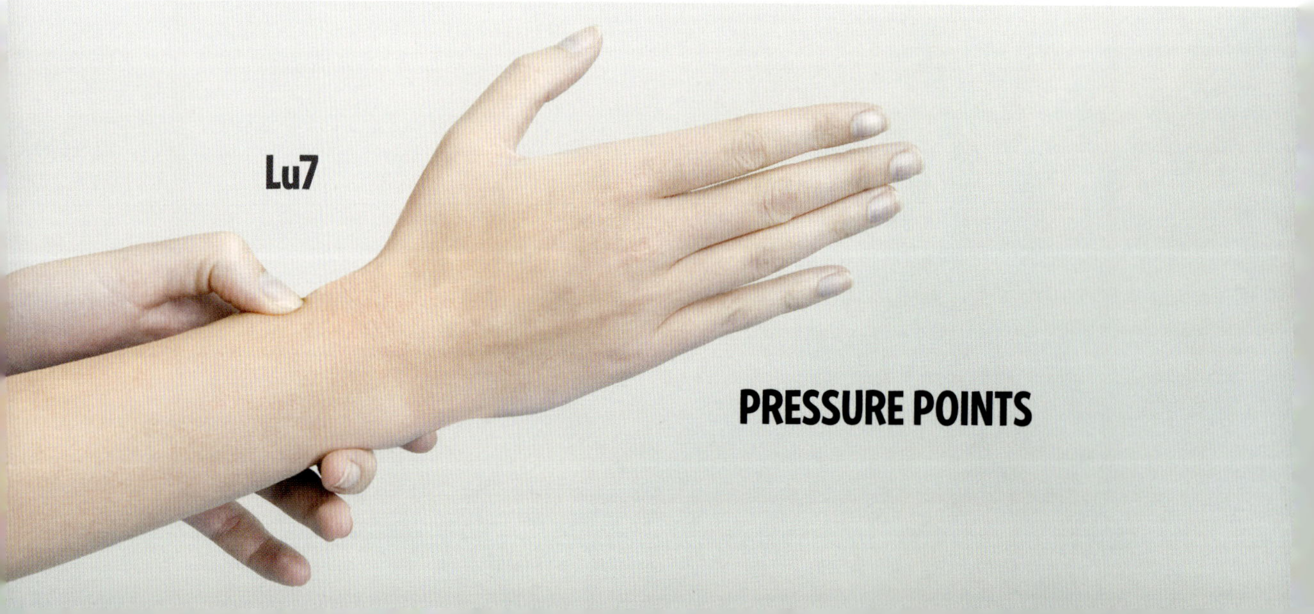

PRESSURE POINTS

IN TRADITIONAL CHINESE MEDICINE

Fatigue, stress, ageing or a long-term illness can deplete qi and blood, leading to an emptying of blood and the stagnation of qi and blood. The tendons and the joints are therefore not properly nourished. Repeated stress on the wrists (carrying heavy weights) or an excess of surrounding humidity can also create a blockage of qi and an accumulation of humidity, causing pain and swelling of the wrist. A climatic attack of wind-cold and prolonged exposure to cold can lead to a stagnation of qi and blood, which causes wrist pain.

AN EXTRA TIP

In a tinted glass bottle with a dropper, mix 30ml (1fl oz) of **copaiba balsam**, 125 drops of **common juniper essential oil**, 250 drops of **katrafay essential oil** and 125 drops of **lemongrass essential oil**. Apply 10 drops on the painful area, two to five times a day.

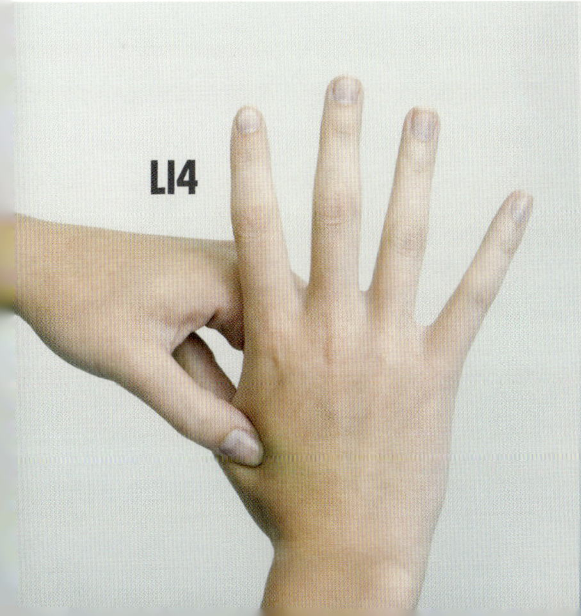

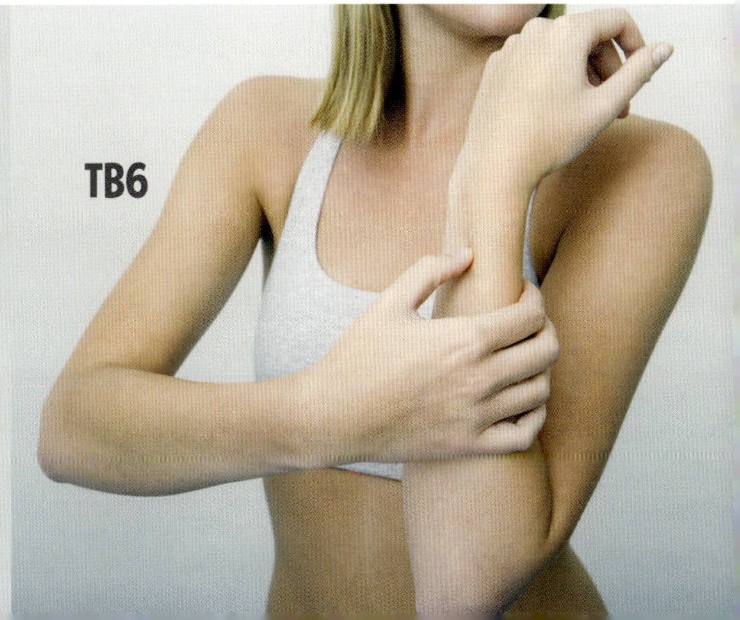

Lumbar pain (lower back) & pain in the legs

Total duration of treatment:
6 MINUTES

Lumbar pain affects the lower back, in the area between the L1 and S3 vertebrae. It is often attributed to kidney disease, osteoarthritis, rheumatoid polyarthritis, a herniated lumbar disc or a spine lesion.

METHOD

- Apply moderate pressure to point **UB40** with your thumb. Maintain this for 2 minutes, then repeat on the opposite side.
- Apply strong pressure to point **GV26** with your thumbnail. Maintain this for 2 minutes. You could also use the tip of a pencil to do this, for increased effectiveness. The pain in response to the stimuli could cause tears, which is a good sign.

PRESSURE POINTS

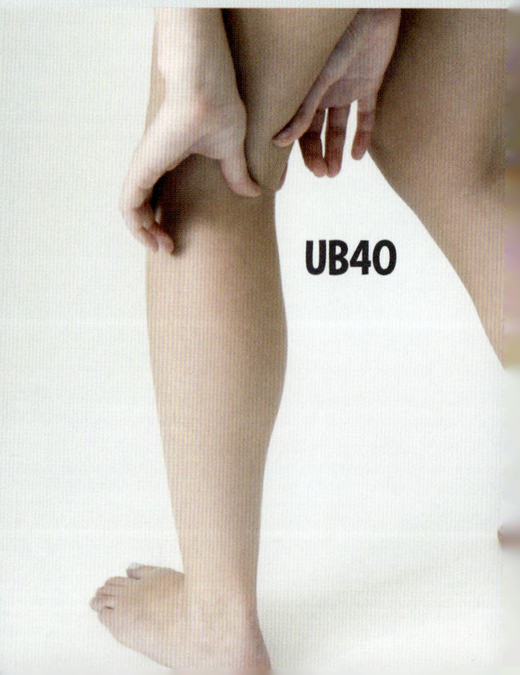

VARIATION

You can also heat the painful area using moxa sticks for 10–15 minutes. This is very effective, as heat clears the blockage.

SOME EXTRA TIPS

- **For a lower back massage:** in a tinted glass bottle with a dropper, mix 15ml (½fl oz) of **St John's Wort (hypericum) macerated oil**, 125 drops of **wintergreen essential oil**, 125 drops of **cineole rosemary essential oil** and 125 drops of **bay laurel essential oil**. Massage 15 drops onto the painful area.
- **For a leg massage:** in a tinted glass bottle with a dropper, mix 30ml (1fl oz) of **macadamia vegetable oil**, 40 drops of **cypress essential oil**, 20 drops of **lavandin essential oil** and 5 drops of **peppermint essential oil**. Massage your legs from the bottom to the top with a few drops of this preparation, two to three times a week.

IN TRADITIONAL CHINESE MEDICINE

Climatic factors (wind, cold, humidity) and stress can lead to lumbar pain, just like a chronically depleted kidney. This can be caused by the stagnation of qi and blood, as well as a muscle strain or an attack of cold on the lumbar region. When unfavourable external climate elements reach the lower limbs, pain is felt in the legs. Wind penetrates into the skin, cold stagnates and humidity is heavy and clinging. This induces stagnation of qi and blood, triggering pain, which gets worse in cold and humid weather. An unbalanced diet (spicy, fatty or sweet foods, dairy products, alcohol) affects the spleen and the stomach, and forms humidity-heat. This descends down the lower limbs and blocks the meridians, creating pain in the legs.

PRESSURE POINTS
Sp6

Generalized aches & pains

Total duration of treatment:
11 MINUTES

As the name indicates, generalized aches and pains affect all parts of the body (muscles, joints, tendons), and are accompanied by fatigue, depression and an aversion to cold. These pains are associated with conditions such as the flu, chronic fatigue syndrome, fibromyalgia and polio.

METHOD
Apply moderate pressure to each point with your thumb. Maintain this for 1 minute, then repeat the procedure on the opposite side.

SOME EXTRA TIPS
- Take a course of **B vitamins**, **magnesium** or opt for a more general formula (without iron or copper). Consult your pharmacist for advice.
- Eliminate gluten and dairy products and limit your consumption of simple carbohydrates (such as white bread, white pasta) and meats (once a week). Opt for foods rich in omega-3s (rapeseed oil, oily fish), oleaginous foods, dark chocolate (at least 72% cocoa solids), legumes, tubers, marrow and chestnuts.

VARIATION
You can also heat the painful areas using a moxa stick (if the areas aren't hot) for 10–15 minutes.

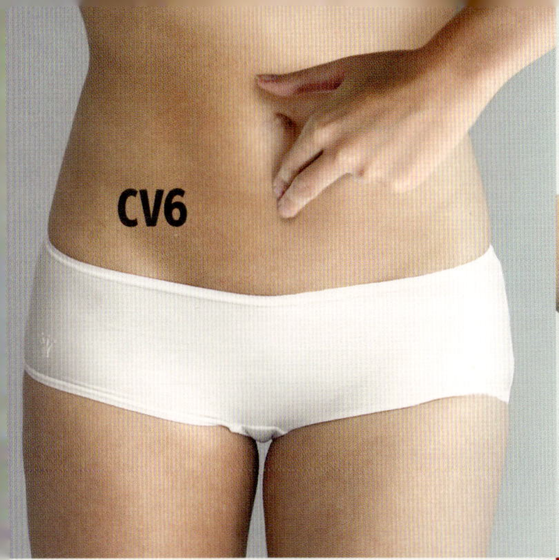

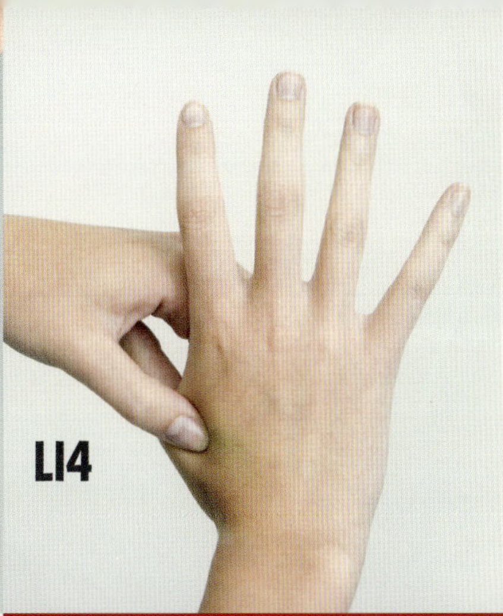

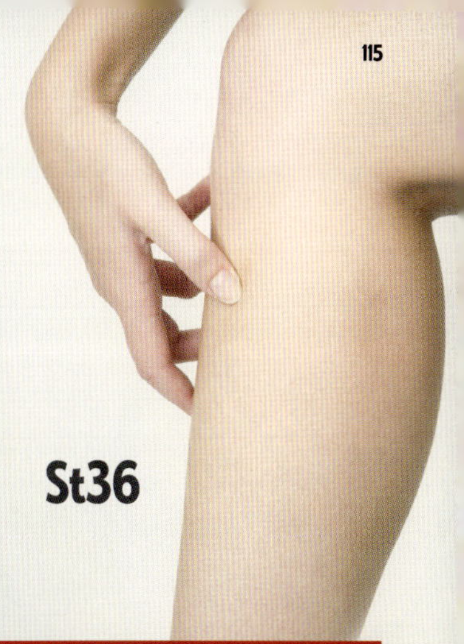

IN TRADITIONAL CHINESE MEDICINE

The attack from climatic factors (wind-cold, wind-humidity, humidity-heat) impedes the free movement of qi and blood, leading to malnutrition of the muscles, tendons and meridians, and resulting in generalized aches and pains. Heightened emotions, stress and burnout can also cause a blockage of the liver's qi, which leads to a slowing down of the blood and body fluids and insufficient nourishment of the muscles, tendons and meridians. An inadequate diet, chronic disease, sexual excess, old age and burnout can also deplete the liver's yin and the kidney's yin and yang. A depletion of qi and blood, as well a stagnation of qi and blood, leads to pain in the whole body.

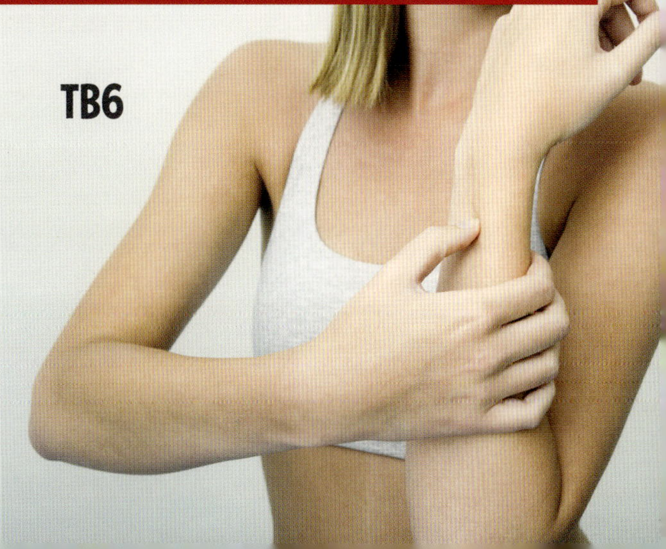

Lumbago

Total duration of treatment:
6 MINUTES

Lumbago is a painful condition most frequently caused by awkward movement. It is identified by a very sharp lumbar pain and a feeling of obstruction in the lumbar spine. Lumbago is the most common manifestation of lumbosacral disc deterioration.

PRESSURE POINTS

GV26

METHOD

- Apply moderate pressure to each point with your thumb. Maintain this for 2 minutes, then repeat the procedure on the opposite side.
- You can strongly stimulate point **GV26** with your nail until it brings on tears, while gently moving your pelvis at the same time.

VARIATION

As a complement, heat the painful area (if the area is not hot) using moxa sticks until it becomes red. Do this once a day for 10–15 minutes until recovery.

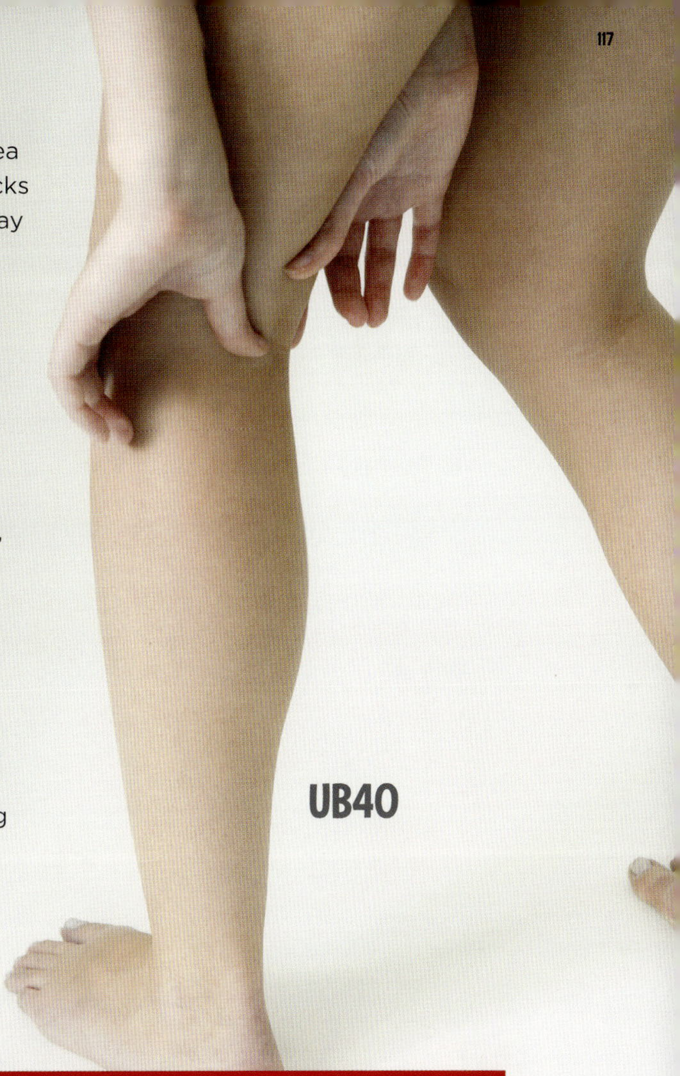

SOME EXTRA TIPS

- In a bottle, mix 15ml (½ fl oz) of **hypericum plant oil**, 75 drops of **helichrysum essential oil**, 75 drops of **lemon eucalyptus essential oil**, 25 drops of **cardamom essential oil**, 25 drops of **ylang-ylang essential oil** and 25 drops of **bay laurel essential oil**. Apply a few drops of this mixture on the painful area, five to six times a day.
- To avoid an attack of cold-humidity in the area, avoid walking barefoot on a cold and damp floor, perspiring too much without changing, staying too long in water or going outside without covering yourself adequately, especially around the stomach and the lower back.

IN TRADITIONAL CHINESE MEDICINE

The lumbar region is the seat of the kidney. The internal branch of the kidney's meridian penetrates into the backbone, which creates the kidney/lumbar region relationship. Lumbago can be triggered when there is an attack of cold-humidity in the area, which obstructs the meridians and the tendino-muscular (sinew) meridians. Excessive sexual activity consumes the essence (Jing) and qi. The kidney, the tissues and the area are undernourished, and lumbago results from the depletion of qi and/or of Jing. A fall or trauma can also cause damage to qi and the blood, leading to lumbago. Limited lumbar movement, and perhaps even an inability to stand straight or lay flat and/or walk, reflect this stagnation of qi and blood.

Toothache

Total duration of treatment:
8 MINUTES

This particularly uncomfortable pain may be accompanied by swelling in the cheeks and headaches, and usually requires a trip to the dentist. But, in the meantime, you can relieve the pain using natural methods.

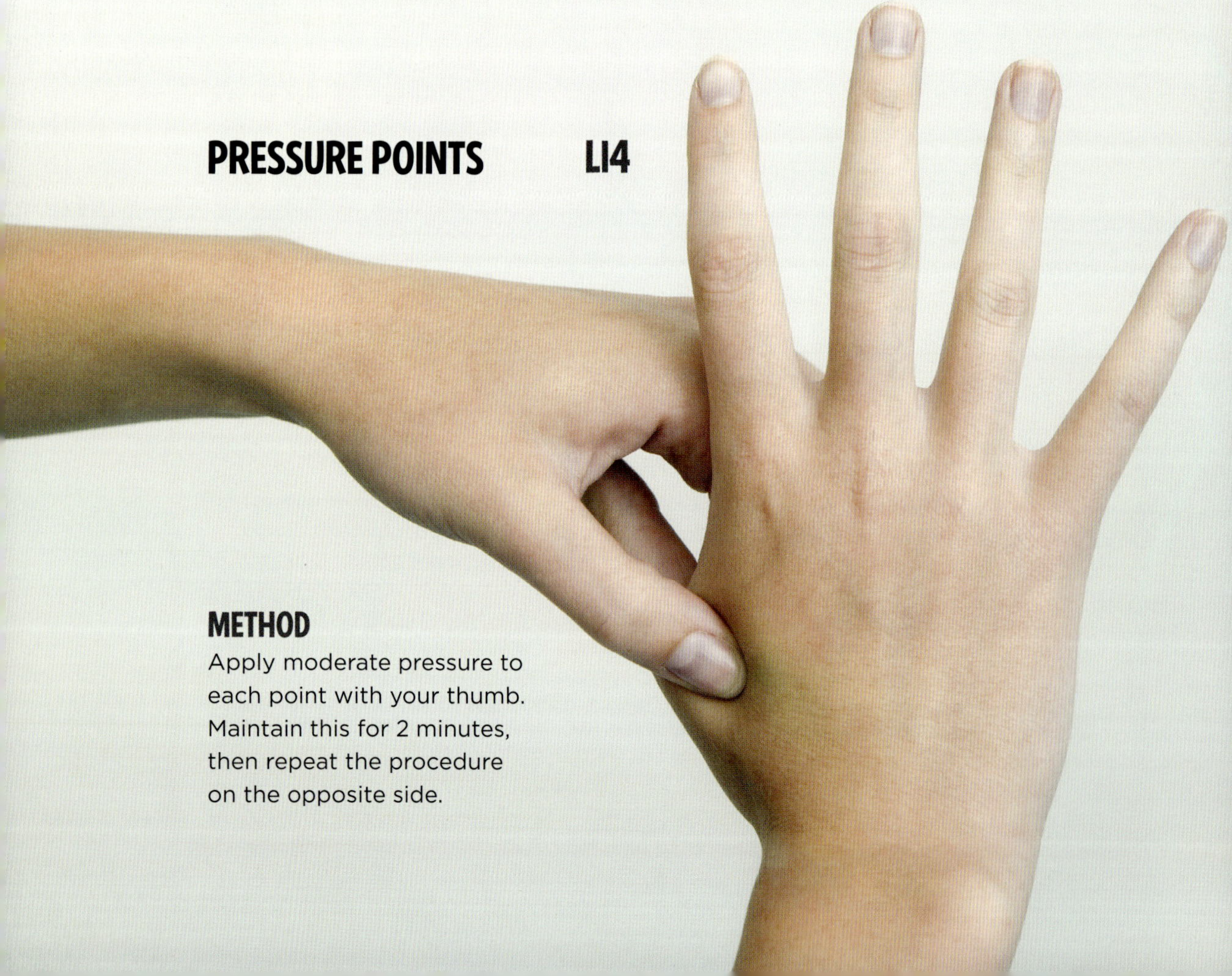

PRESSURE POINTS

LI4

METHOD

Apply moderate pressure to each point with your thumb. Maintain this for 2 minutes, then repeat the procedure on the opposite side.

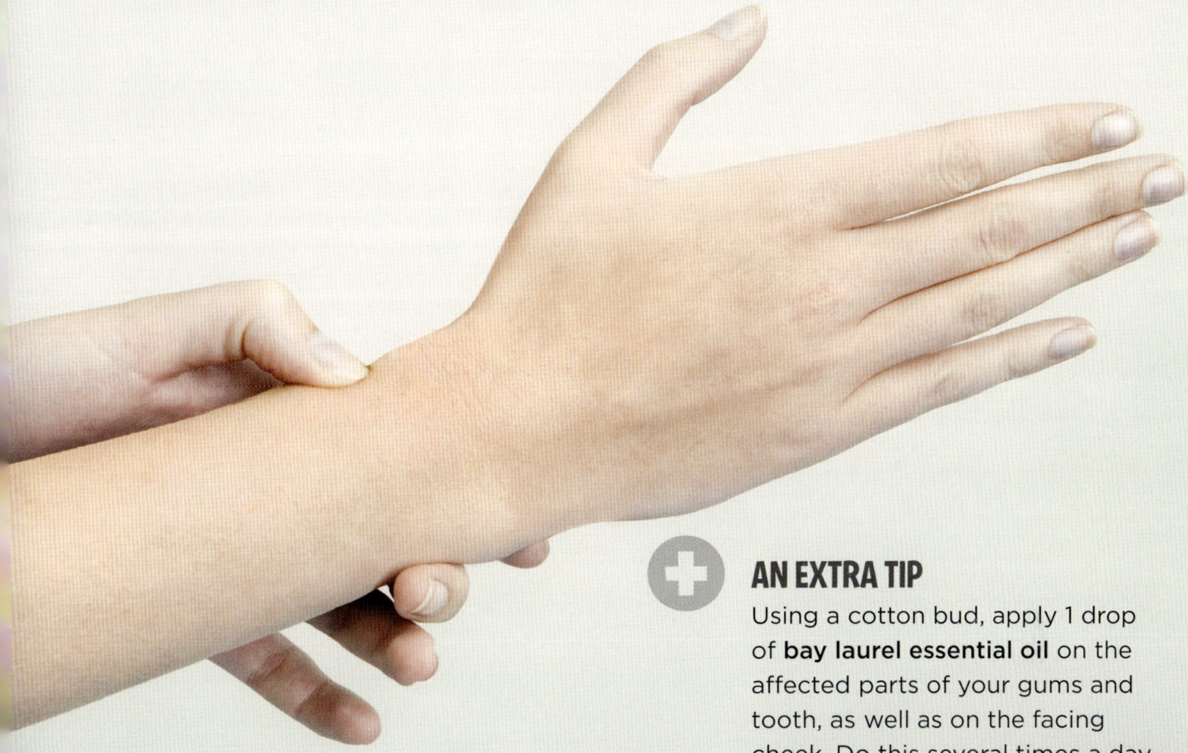

AN EXTRA TIP

Using a cotton bud, apply 1 drop of **bay laurel essential oil** on the affected parts of your gums and tooth, as well as on the facing cheek. Do this several times a day, while waiting to consult a dentist.

IN TRADITIONAL CHINESE MEDICINE

The meridians of the stomach and the large intestine are both connected to the teeth. The stomach enters the lower teeth and the large intestine enters the upper teeth. A climatic attack of wind-cold or wind-heat reaches the top of the body where all the yang meridians meet, and this affects the teeth. The movement of qi and blood in the mouth accelerates with heat and slows down with cold, creating pain. An excess of spicy and hot foods, alcohol, dairy products and sugar can also create an accumulation of heat, which, via the meridians, rises and results in dental pain. The kidney governs the bones as well as the teeth (which are an extension of the bones). In cases of depletion of the kidney's Jing-essence, the teeth will be affected. A fire of the kidney (yin depletion), linked to old age, stress, sexual excess and masturbation, excessive loss of blood during periods, alcohol or drug abuse, or lack of sleep, can also affect the teeth, not forgetting inadequate oral hygiene, which promotes the proliferation of bacteria.

Headache (migraine)

Total duration of treatment:
14 MINUTES

Migraines (headaches) occur frequently: they are one of the main reasons for seeking medical advice. Their causes can be varied.

METHOD

Apply moderate pressure to each point with your thumb. Maintain this for 2 minutes, then repeat the procedure on the opposite side.

AN EXTRA TIP

In a tinted glass bottle with a dropper, mix 15ml (½ fl oz) of **hypericum plant oil**, 50 drops of **bay laurel essential oil**, 50 drops of **wild mint essential oil**, 50 drops of **tropical basil essential oil**, 25 drops of **wintergreen essential oil** and 50 drops of **ylang-ylang essential oil**. Apply 3 drops of this mixture on the forehead and temples. Repeat as often as you like, several times a day.

PRESSURE POINTS

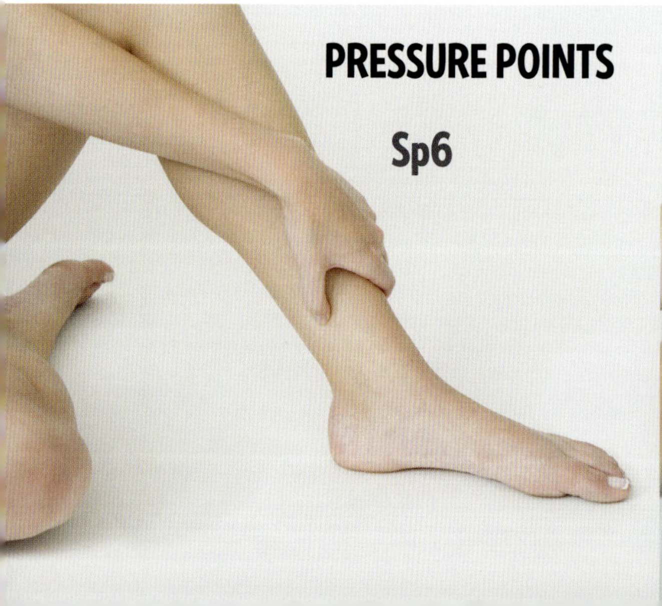

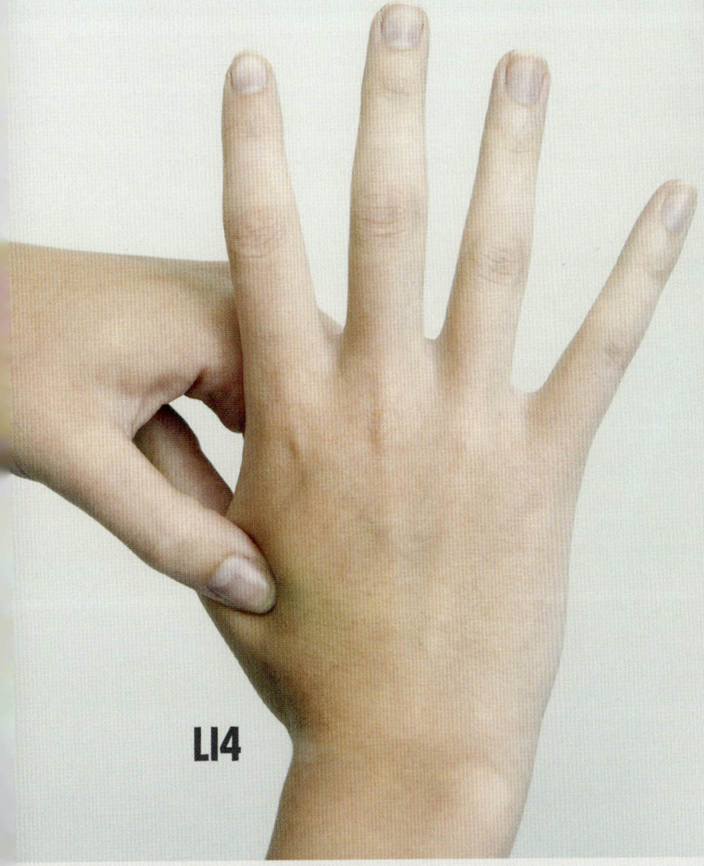

IN TRADITIONAL CHINESE MEDICINE

The head is the meeting place of all the yangs and the area of the six yang meridians. The qi and blood of the organs and bowels pass through the head. Internal damage can create disharmony in the head's qi and blood, as well as stagnation of qi in the meridians, resulting in pain. Migraines may be caused by external factors, connected with an attack from wind, which reaches the meridians from the upper part of the head. The cause may also be internal, resulting from an excessive rising of the liver's yang or the depletion of qi and blood.

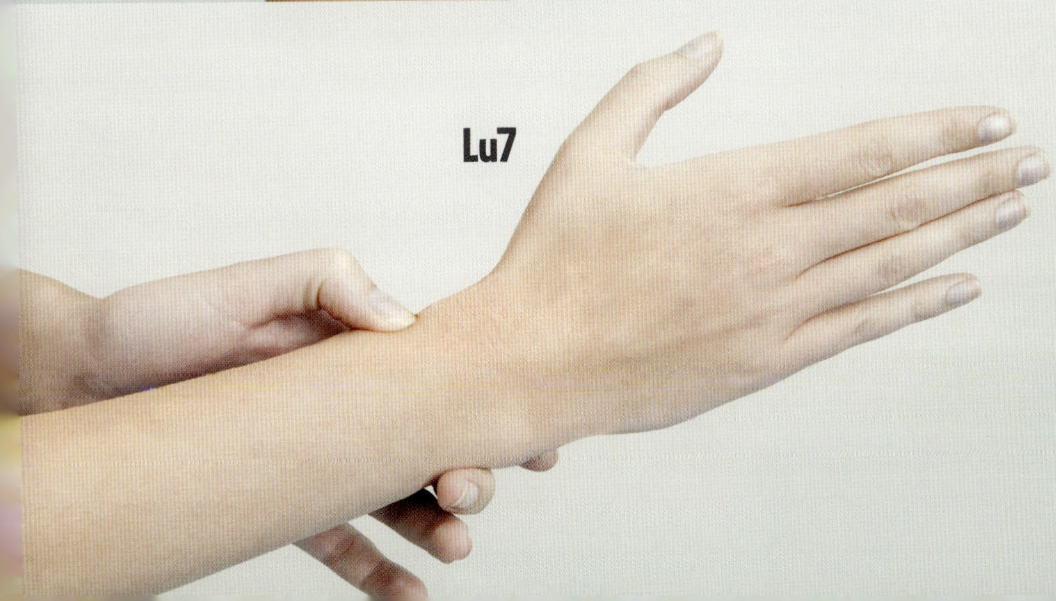

Sciatica

Total duration of treatment:
8 MINUTES

This sharp pain is linked to irritation of the sciatic nerve. It is often accompanied by lumbago (lumbosciatica).

METHOD

Apply moderate pressure to each point with your thumb. Maintain this for 2 minutes, then repeat the procedure on the opposite side.

PRESSURE POINTS

IN TRADITIONAL CHINESE MEDICINE

Sciatica is associated with an obstruction of the meridians due to malnutrition from the depletion of qi and blood linked to the body's chronic depletion. As the qi and the blood are no longer nourishing the meridians, this leads to diminishing motor function and pain. Physical trauma (falls, accidents, blows) and the penetration of wind, cold or humidity can also cause strong pains from the stagnation of qi and blood. In such cases, the ailment is of the 'abundance' type, and manifests through pain that can be severe.

SOME EXTRA TIPS

- In a bottle, mix 15ml (½ fl oz) of **hypericum plant oil**, 50 drops of **helichrysum essential oil**, 50 drops of **savoury thyme essential oil**, 50 drops of **ylang-ylang essential oil**, 50 drops of **wintergreen essential oil**, 25 drops of **roman chamomile essential oil**, 50 drops of **peppermint essential oil** and 25 drops of **bay laurel essential oil**. Apply a few drops of this mixture to the painful area five times a day.
- Stress management is also important: the tensions created by stress contribute directly to pain and muscular contractures.

Stiff neck (torticolis)

Total duration of treatment:
10 MINUTES

Torticolis is a contracture of the neck muscles, which is involuntary and impossible to control, causing a rotation and inclination of the head. It is accompanied by stiffness, sharp pain and a deviation of the head to one side.

METHOD

Apply moderate pressure to each point with your thumb. Maintain this for 2 minutes, then repeat the procedure on the opposite side.

VARIATION

As a complement, heat the painful area using moxa sticks until it becomes red.

GV26

PRESSURE POINTS

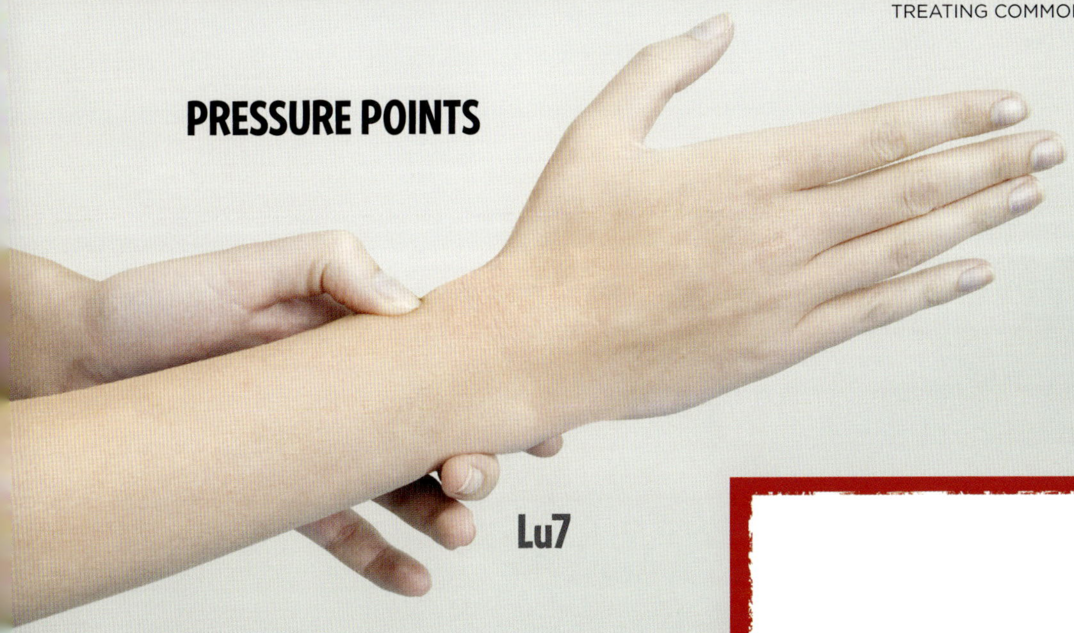

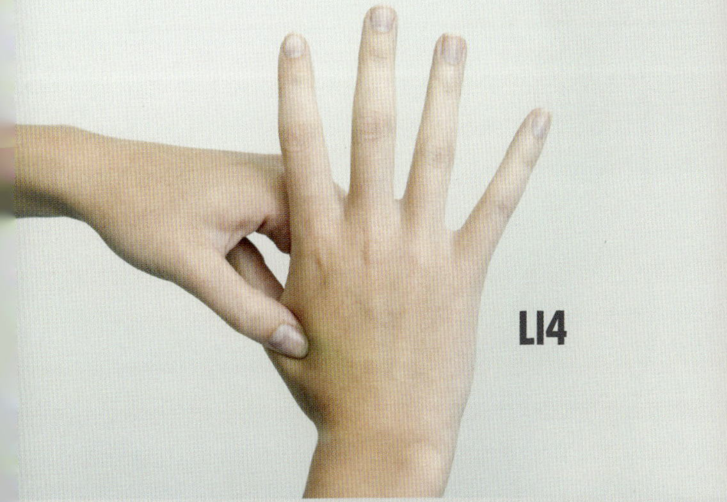

IN TRADITIONAL CHINESE MEDICINE

A stiff neck is caused by tendon injury in the neck, which can occur following an awkward sleeping position, for example, or disharmony in the meridians' local qi caused by an attack of wind-cold on the nape of the neck and the back. This results in a stagnation of qi and/or blood and/or wind-cold-humidity obstructing its free movement to reach the tendons.

SOME EXTRA TIPS

In a 50ml (1¾fl oz) bottle, mix 10ml (⅓fl oz) of **copaiba balsam**, 10ml of **wintergreen essential oil**, 10ml of **lemon eucalyptus**, 88 drops of **cineole rosemary essential oil** and 12 drops of **clove essential oil**. Apply a few drops of this mixture using prolonged application on the base of the neck several times a day, along with moxibustion.

Absence of periods

Total duration of treatment:
14 MINUTES

The absence of periods can be primary (for a young woman of 16 or more, who has never had a period) or secondary (for a woman who already has her periods, when this absence lasts for more than 3 months).

CAUTION!

Do not try the essential-oil massage (opposite) if there is a history of hormone-dependent cancer, or if you suffer from epilepsy.

METHOD

Apply moderate pressure to each point with your thumb. Maintain this for 2 minutes, then repeat the procedure on the opposite side.

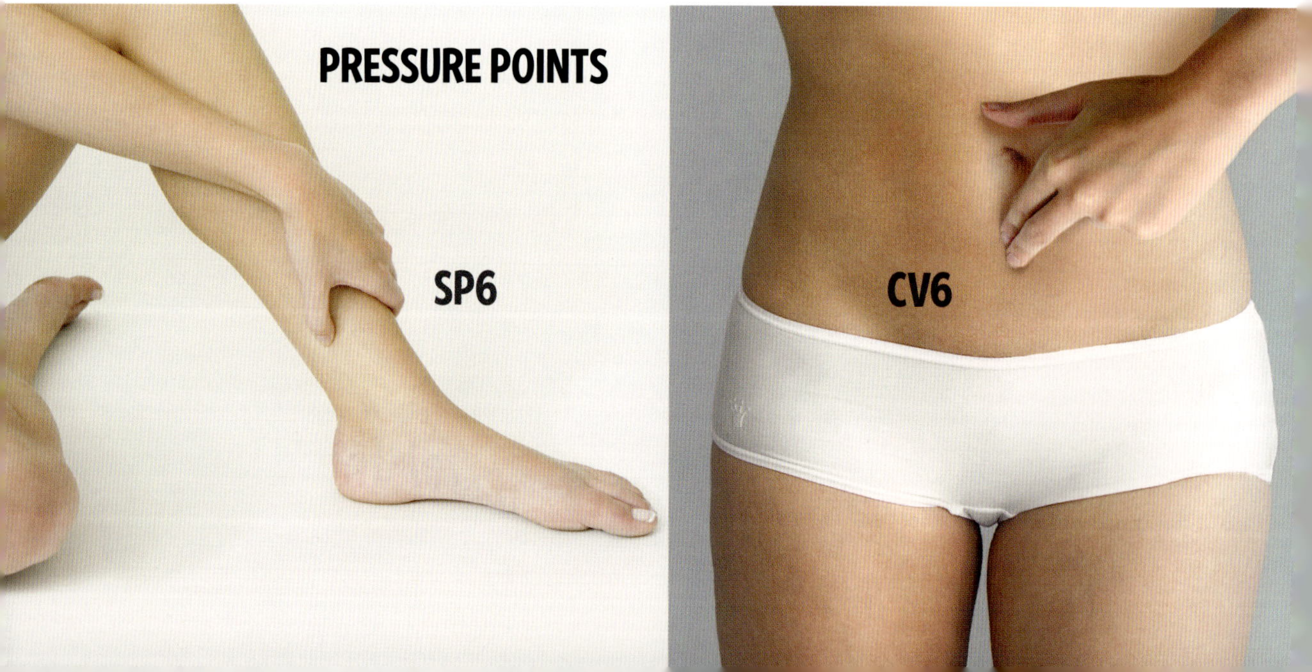

AN EXTRA TIP

In a tinted glass bottle with a dropper, mix 27ml (just under 1fl oz) of **macadamia vegetable oil**, 45 drops of **clary sage essential oil** and 30 drops of **garden sage essential oil**. Massage 4 drops of this mixture onto the stomach, morning and evening, until your periods reappear.

IN TRADITIONAL CHINESE MEDICINE

This imbalance is mainly associated with a state of depletion, more rarely with a state of abundance. Generally, it is due to the stagnation of blood or the depletion of blood. Emotional shocks, anger and frustrations lead to a blockage of the liver. This leads to a stagnation of qi and blood, which obstructs the tubes of the uterus, preventing the flow of menstrual blood. A unbalanced nutritional diet, as well as fatigue, damages the spleen's qi, which causes a reduction in the source of production and general transformation. Chronic diseases can also affect the blood and yin. Excessive sexual relations or repeated pregnancies may also tire the liver and the kidney, leading to a loss of the essence (Jing) and of blood, which has the effect of blocking periods.

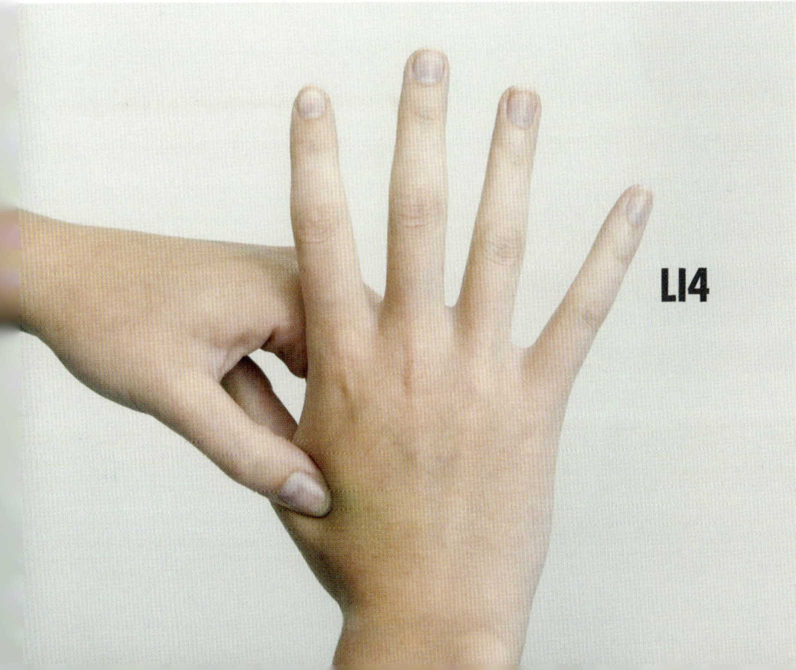

Childbirth (delivery)

Total duration of treatment:
VARIABLE

Labour in childbirth is expected when the mother has gone past the full pregnancy term (41 weeks) by a few days (6 maximum). Other medical reasons connected to the mother's health can also push health professionals to consider labour before term, such as the risk of pre-eclampsia (associated with arterial hypertension, proteinuria and weight gain with oedema), gestational diabetes, an abnormal position of the foetus, infection of the amniotic fluid or even miscarriage.

PRESSURE POINTS

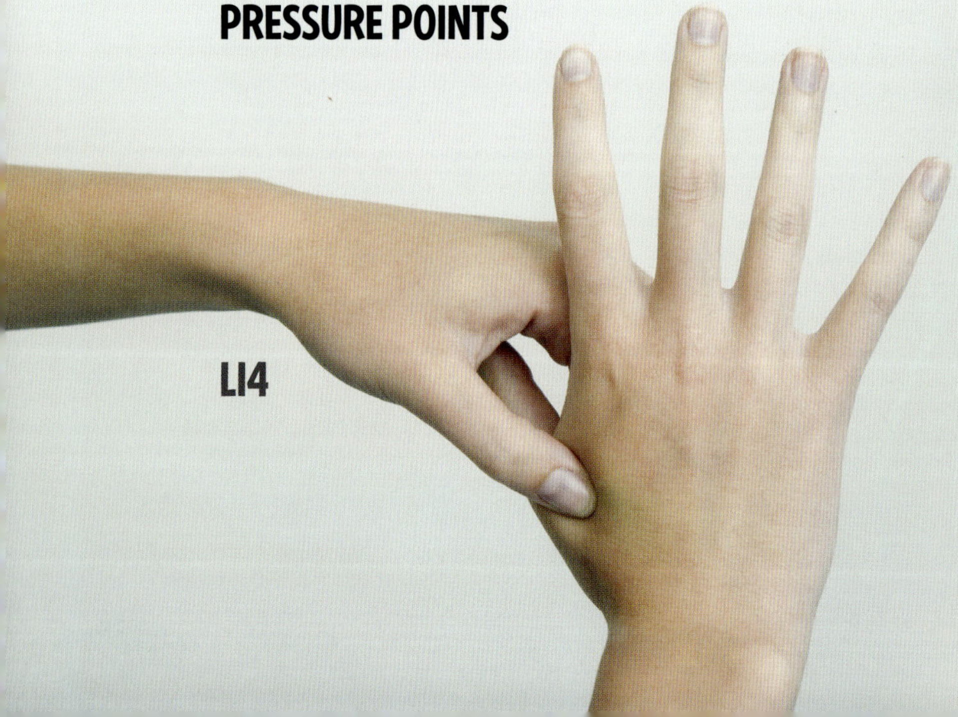

LI4

METHOD

Heat the points in alternation with a moxa stick, until delivery.

SOME EXTRA TIPS

- Try to relax as much as possible, in order to help with the effort of delivery.
- Acupuncture can also be an effective aid for inducing labour.

IN TRADITIONAL CHINESE MEDICINE

When labour does not start, it is often thought that this is due to a constitutional deficiency of qi, blood and Jing (the kidney's essence), which leads to weakness of uterine contractions or stagnation of qi and blood.

Bed-wetting & urinary incontinence

Total duration of treatment:
20 MINUTES

Bed-wetting is defined as involuntary and unconscious urination without damage to the urinary system, happening most frequently during sleep. This disorder affects almost 10 per cent of children, especially boys. Urinary incontinence mostly affects women, and its frequency increases with age.

METHOD

- Apply moderate pressure to each point (except **CV6**) with your thumb for 2 minutes. Repeat the procedure on the opposite side.
- Heat point **CV6** with a moxa stick for around 10 minutes, until the area becomes red.

PRESSURE POINTS

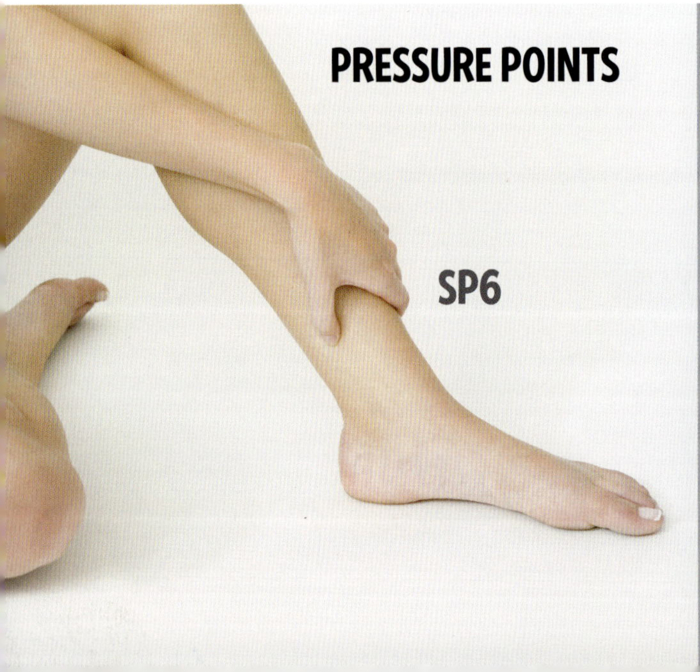

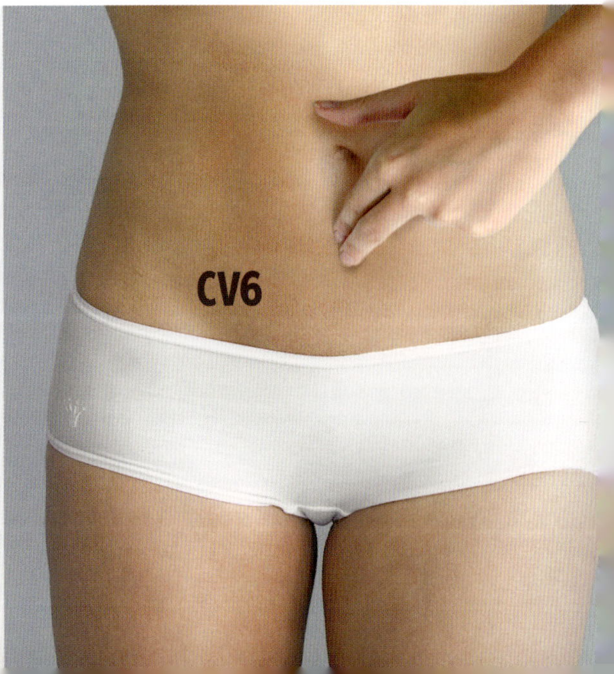

SOME EXTRA TIPS

- For obvious reasons, avoid drinking too much before going to bed.
- Avoid all stress involving overstimulation of the kidney's energy: overly long walks, standing for long periods of time, stamping, sexual excess ...
- In a 10ml (⅓ fl oz) tinted glass bottle with a dropper, mix 8ml (¼ fl oz) of **apricot kernel oil** and 50 drops of **cypress essential oil**. Massage 10 drops onto the lower stomach and the lower back at bedtime. **Caution**: not to be done if previously diagnosed with hormone-dependent cancer.

IN TRADITIONAL CHINESE MEDICINE

The kidney's yang energy manages the lower orifices. When there is a weakening or deficiency of this energy, the capacity to retain and control liquids is lower. For children, this weakening/deficiency may be linked to a weak hereditary energy of the kidney. With older people, the kidney's yang energy diminishes with time, which is why a deficiency of the kidney leads to bladder dysfunction.

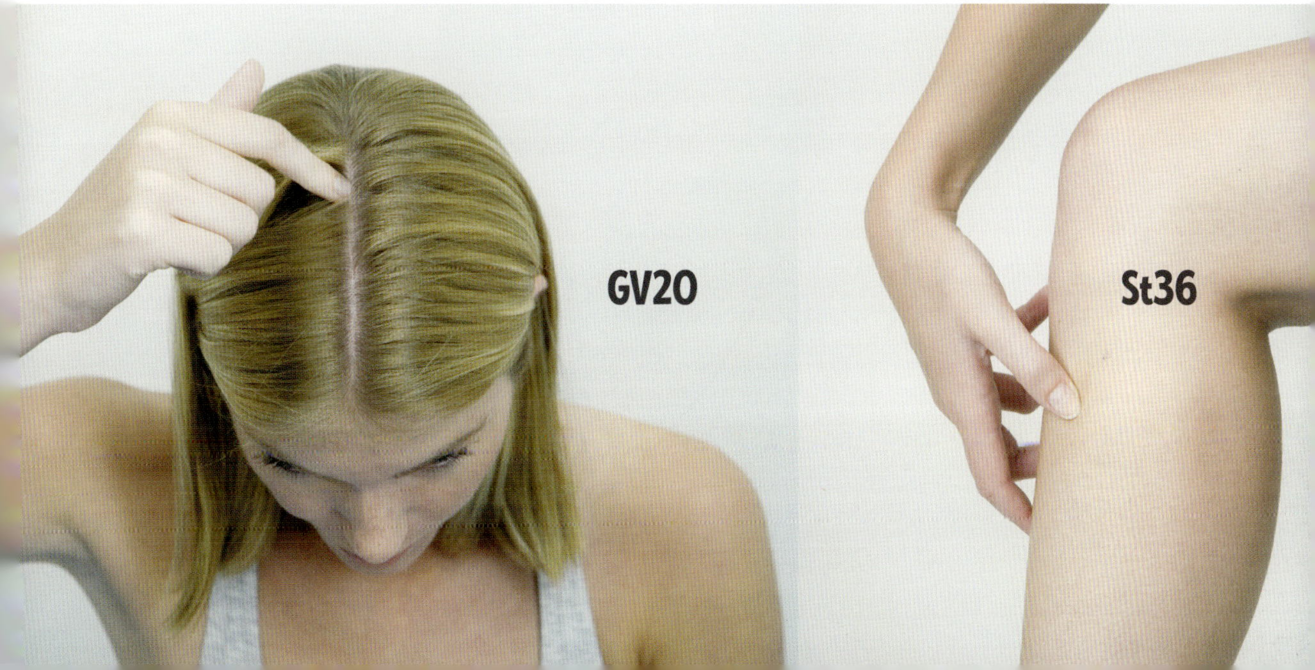

Erectile dysfunction

Total duration of treatment:
10 MINUTES

Erectile dysfunction, or problems with erection, refers to cases of a persistent inability to achieve or maintain an erection sufficiently for a fulfilling sexual relationship.

METHOD

- Apply moderate pressure to each point with your thumb. Maintain this for 2 minutes, then repeat the procedure on the opposite side.
- You could also heat these points for 15 minutes each until the area becomes slightly red. For point **CV6**, heat until there is a soft diffusion of heat on the lower stomach.

PRESSURE POINTS

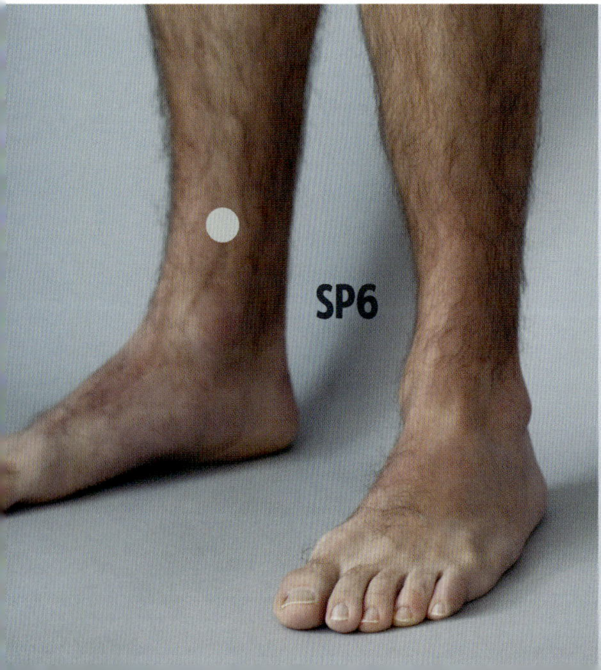

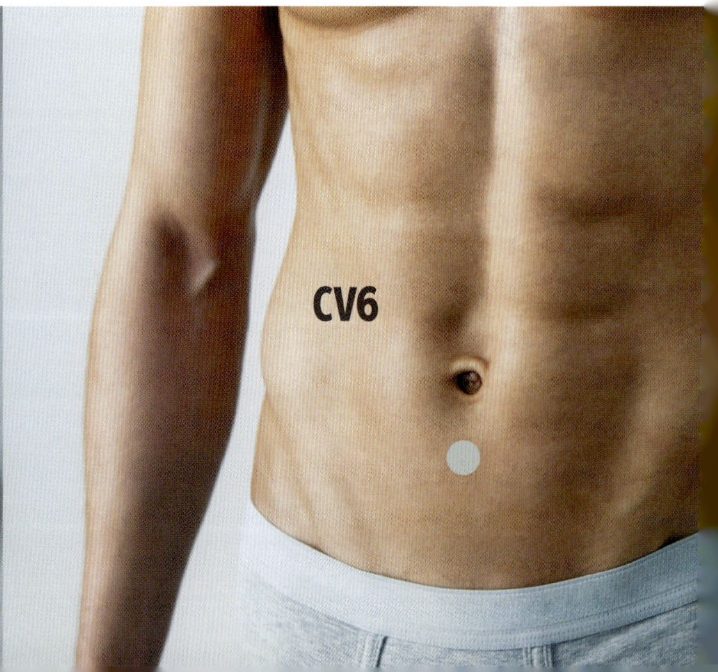

SOME EXTRA TIPS

- Taking **L-Arginine** (a semi-essential amino acid) is effective for stimulating sexual vigour, as it promotes the blood surge required for erection. The correct dose is 2g to 5g per day. **Caution**: do not use if there is a history of heart attack.
- In a tinted glass bottle with a dropper, mix 6ml (⅕ fl oz) of **apricot kernel plant oil**, 75 drops of **Siam wood essential oil** and 12 drops of **bergamot mint essential oil**. Apply 10 drops on the lower stomach and the lower back, mornings and evenings, for 21 days.

VARIATION

You could also heat the entire lower stomach and lumbar areas, to tone the whole body. This area is in direct contact with the body's yang energy. This is very effective in restoring general vitality during convalescence and also as a preventative measure, for regular health maintenance throughout life.

IN TRADITIONAL CHINESE MEDICINE

Erection is linked to a healthy replenishing of the cavernous body of the penis. This depends on the good overall movement of qi and blood. The abundance of the liver's qi helps the penis to dilate. Problems with erection, or its absence, come from a decrease in the liver's yang; the liver meridian is linked to the external genital organ. In the case of a deficiency in the liver's yang, there is abundance of yin and of internal cold-humidity. If the liver's energy is blocked, the rise of yang and the dispersion of qi are impeded, leading to a disturbance in erectile function because the penis is not stimulated and heated. The liver is the regulator of stress and the emotions. It likes fluidity and does not tolerate frustration. Emotional blockages may also result in the dysfunction of the genital organs.

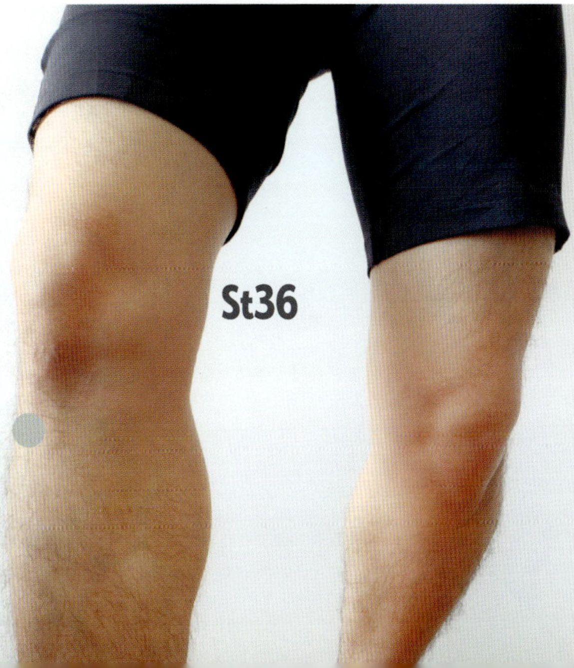

Painful periods

Total duration of treatment:
15 MINUTES

Regular pains can occur before, during or after menstruation. They can be located in the lower stomach or the sacral area, and sometimes extend to the lower limbs. In serious cases, they can be accompanied by nausea, vomiting and even loss of consciousness.

METHOD

Apply moderate pressure to each point with your thumb. Maintain this for 3 minutes, then repeat the procedure on the opposite side. Repeat several times a day. This can be done as a preventative measure (two to three days before the start of your period) and for the entire duration of your period.

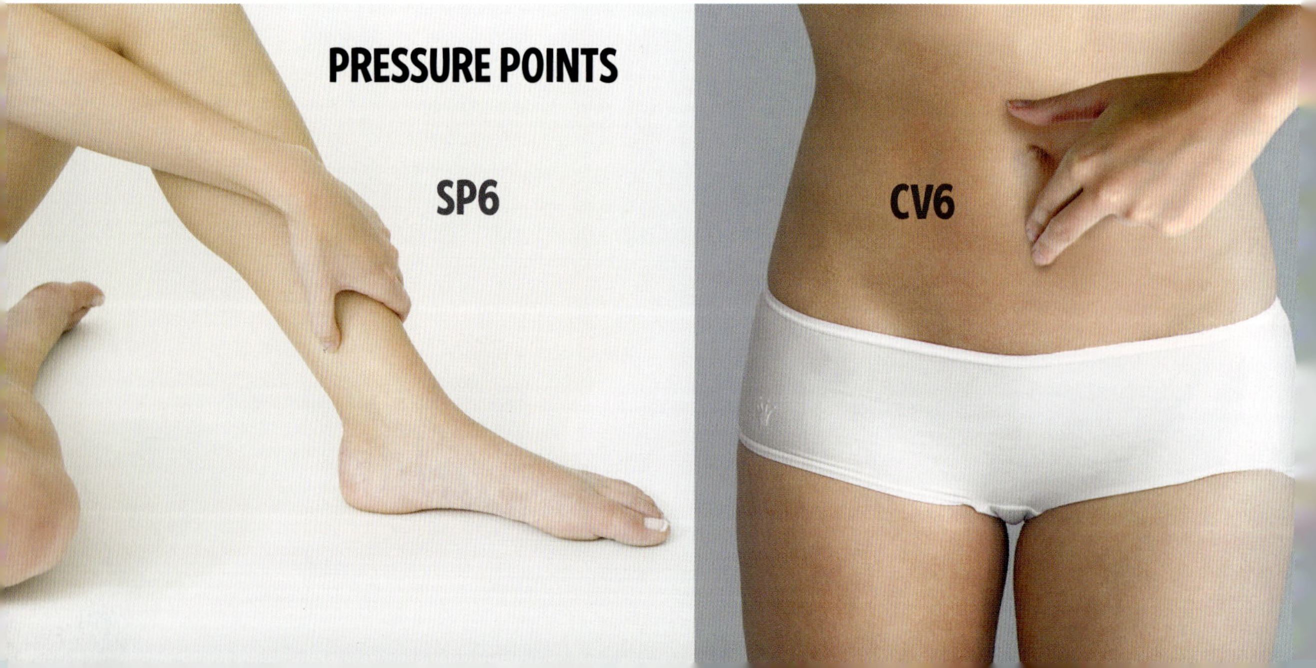

VARIATION

As a complement, you can also heat the lower stomach area with a moxa stick, until the skin becomes red, or place a hot-water bottle on the painful area.

AN EXTRA TIP

In a tinted glass bottle, mix 50 drops of **tarragon essential oil**, 50 drops of **roman chamomile essential oil**, 25 drops of **ylang-ylang essential oil** and 25 drops of **sage essential oil**. Apply 5 drops of this mixture on the lower abdomen five times a day during the acute phase, or twice a day as a preventative measure, two days before the start of your period.

IN TRADITIONAL CHINESE MEDICINE

Normal menstrual periods are painless periods, where the blood is abundant and circulates properly. Good blood circulation depends on the free movement of the liver's qi and the qi of the Penetrating Vessel (Chong Mai) – one of the eight extraordinary vessels. The liver, the Penetrating Vessel and the Conception Vessel (Ren Mai) are responsible for the physiology of menstruation. During the premenstrual phase, yang rises and the liver's qi circulates to prepare for the blood's movement during periods. If the liver's qi stagnates, this leads to premenstrual pains; if the liver's blood stagnates, this leads to pains during periods. Stagnation is the most significant pathologic factor for painful periods. Emotional tension is also one of the principal factors of painful periods (in addition to cold and internal humidity), because anger and frustration create a blockage in the liver. This slows down the circulation of the liver's qi and leads to the blood stagnating in the uterus, creating pain.

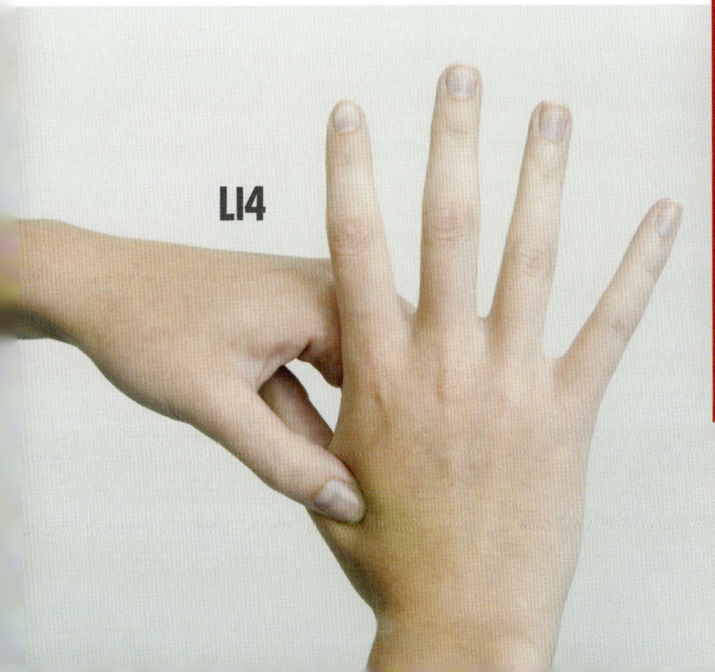

Urinary problems

Total duration of treatment:
9 MINUTES

This term includes the conditions called *lin* in Chinese clinical terminology, such as pollakiuria (excessive frequency of urination) and dysuria (difficult or painful urination).

METHOD

Apply moderate pressure to each point with your thumb. Maintain this for 3 minutes, then repeat the procedure on the opposite side.

AN EXTRA TIP

Acupressure can help to relieve urinary conditions while waiting to consult a specialist, who can determine the cause and offer an appropriate treatment.

IN TRADITIONAL CHINESE MEDICINE

An unbalanced diet (excessive fatty, sugary and fried foods, and abuse of alcohol) creates an accumulation of humidity-heat. Urine gets concentrated and kidney stones are formed, damaging the kidney and the bladder or the ureter. Anger and frustration cause a blockage of the liver's qi, which transforms into fire in the lower body and disturbs the bladder's function, giving rise to dysuria. An excess of sexual activity or intellectual and physical stress leads to a depletion of the liver's qi or a collapse of the spleen's qi, causing dysuria triggered by fatigue.

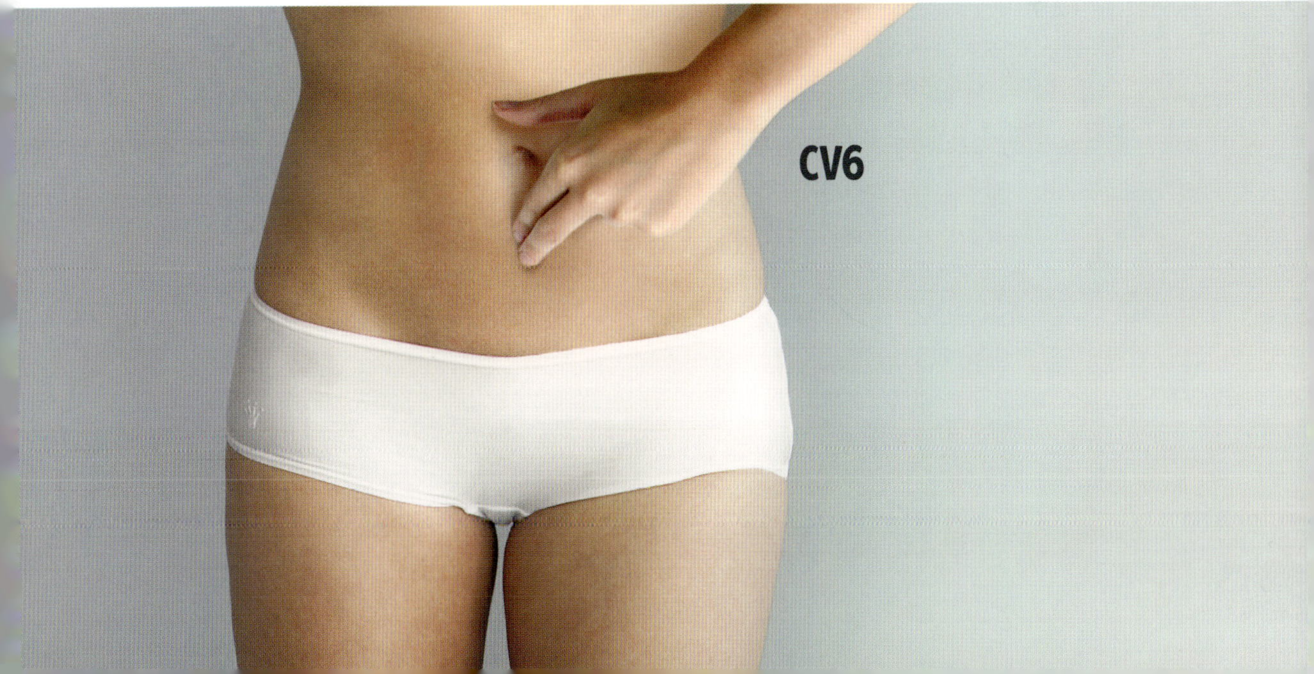

Epilepsy

Total duration of treatment:
3 MINUTES

Epilepsy is a chronic disease characterized by repeated seizure attacks resulting from violent electrical discharges from a group of the brain's nerve cells. The attacks manifest in the form of convulsions of the limbs, sharp cries, a rolling back of the eyes and foaming saliva.

METHOD

Apply moderate pressure on the point of the affected person with your index finger. Maintain this for 3 minutes. You can also use the tip of a pencil for a more powerful effect.

AN EXTRA TIP

Try acupuncture, as a complementary treatment.

IN TRADITIONAL CHINESE MEDICINE

Fear and fright can bring about an internal attack in the free circulation and movements of qi, inducing a depletion of the kidney and liver, causing an internal wind. An inadequate diet (raw, cold, fried, spicy and fatty foods) damages the spleen and the stomach. When the digestive functions are impeded, humidity transforms into phlegm and obstructs Shen. The latter, which is associated with a rising qi, triggers epilepsy.

PRESSURE POINT
GV26

Fatigue

Total duration of treatment:
10 MINUTES

Fatigue is a condition resulting from physiological or psychological stress, leading to reduced physical or cognitive performance. Physiological fatigue is reversible with rest, which restores a normal level of function.

METHOD

Apply moderate pressure to each point with your thumb. Maintain this for 2 minutes, then repeat the procedure on the opposite side.

PRESSURE POINTS

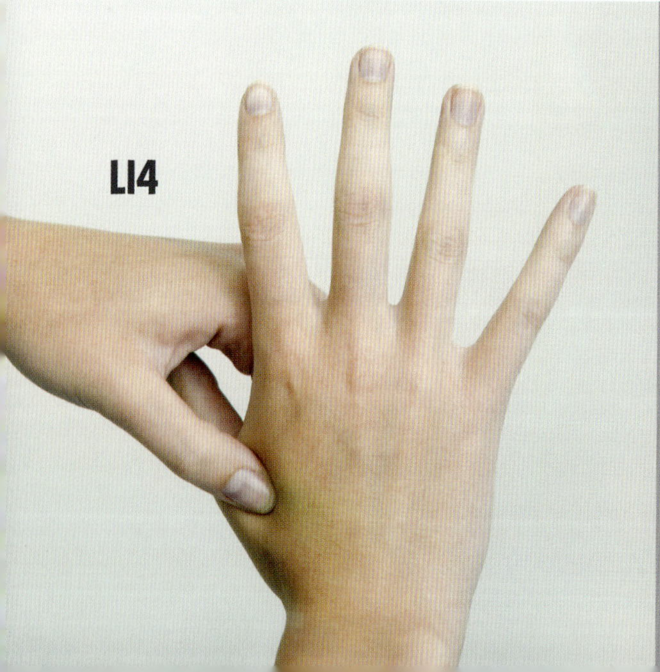

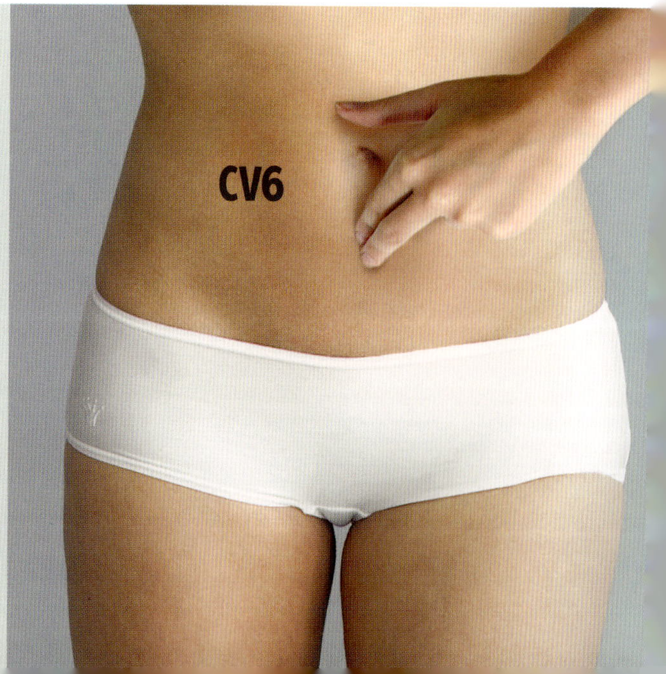

SOME EXTRA TIPS

- Apply 2 to 4 drops of **black spruce essential oil** on your adrenals (the hollow in the middle of your back), mornings and evenings for three weeks. **Caution**: not to be done on pregnant women, children and those suffering from a hormone-dependent cancer.
- You can also mix in a bottle 190 drops of **ravintsara essential oil**, 60 drops of **thyme thujanol essential oil**, 40 drops of **Indian lemongrass essential oil**, 40 drops of **sage essential oil** and 50 drops of **tea tree essential oil**. Apply 15 drops of this mixture on your back, morning, noon and evening, for five days. Repeat ten days later.

IN TRADITIONAL CHINESE MEDICINE

The lung is the master of energy. It governs qi, the essential substance that helps us maintain life's activities. It rules over the energy of the entire body and the energy of respiration. The spleen and the stomach ensure the original source of vital motor energy, producing energy and blood in the body. Fatigue is due to an imbalance in the spleen and the lung; these are the two main organs to treat in cases of fatigue – the spleen for depletion of yang, and the lung for depletion of yin. Both can lead to depletion of the kidney's yang or yin, and the depletion of yang can lead to a depletion of yin, and vice versa.

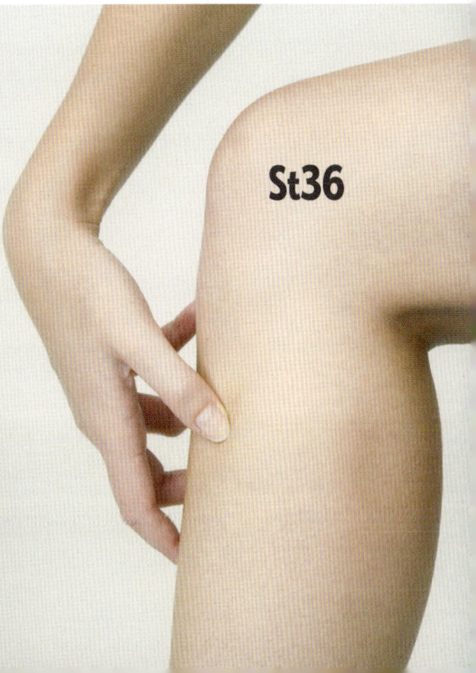

Memory problems

Total duration of treatment:
12 MINUTES

Problems with memory can be linked to many factors: depression, dementia, Alzheimer's and other neurodegenerative diseases, side effects from certain medications, stroke and head injury, as well as anxiety, stress or ageing. Alcoholism and drug use also cause irreparable damage to the neurons and contribute to premature deterioration of the brain and mind.

METHOD

Apply moderate pressure to each point with your index finger for 2 minutes. Repeat the procedure on the opposite side.

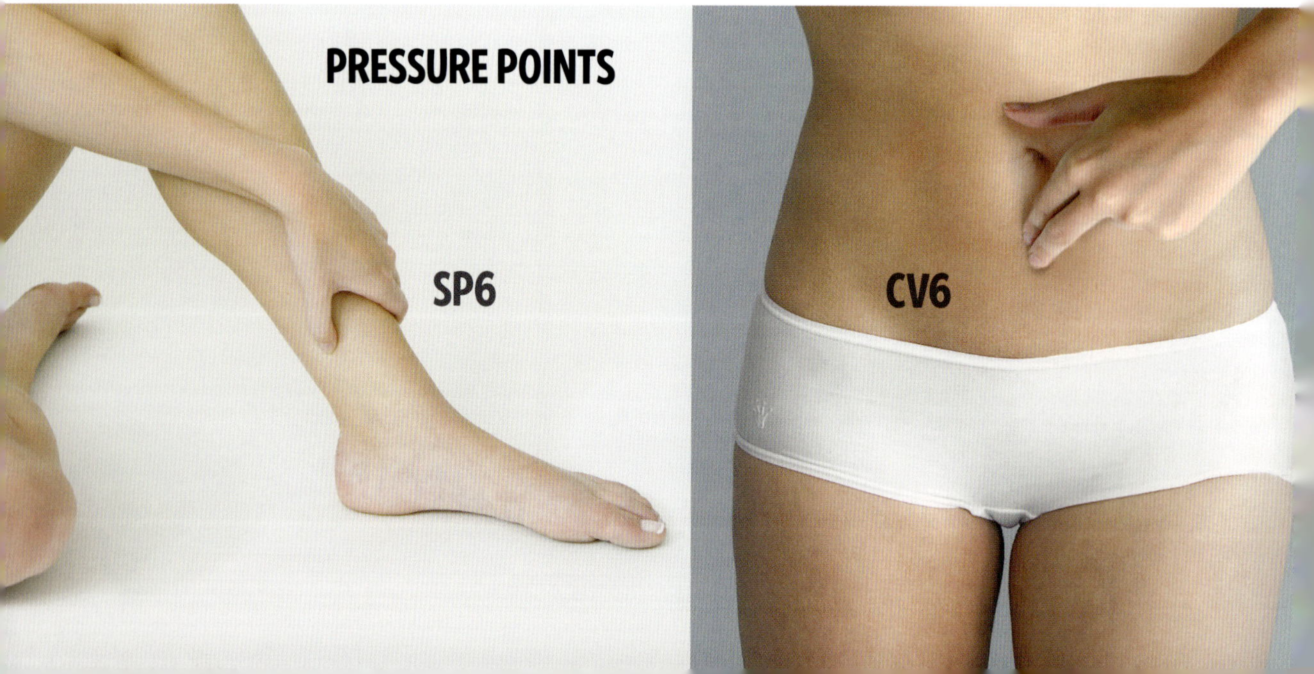

SOME EXTRA TIPS

- Opt for a healthy diet, rich in essential amino acids, omega-3s, minerals and vitamins. Good fats are particularly important in protecting the brain. They are found in oily fish, oleaginous fruits, flaxseed oil and rapeseed oil. The consumption of organic virgin coconut oil, avocado oil and olive oil is also very beneficial.
- Avoid gluten, as it's hard to digest and creates inflammation even in neurons.
- Apply 1 to 2 drops of **damask rose essential oil** on your wrists and inhale deeply. Do this five times in a row, and repeat several times a day.

IN TRADITIONAL CHINESE MEDICINE

The brain is the sea of marrow (spinal marrow and bone marrow). These are the quintessence of the kidney's energy, the seat of the human body's activities. There is a relationship between the kidney and the brain: the weakening of the kidney leads directly to a weakness of the brain and, consequently, of memory. With age, the kidney's essence runs out, and the production of energy falls due to weakness in the digestive system. All this, together with a lack of intellectual and physical exercise, results in fewer nutrients being supplied to the brain, causing it to function less well.

Palpitations

Total duration of treatment:
8 MINUTES

Palpitations are identified as the sensation of the heart beating faster, or in a less regular way, than normal. They can result from great effort, strong emotion or a rush of anxiety, or could be a sign of a problem with the heart rate. In such cases, they may be accompanied by insomnia, memory problems, tinnitus and dizziness.

METHOD

Apply moderate pressure to each point with your thumb. Maintain this for 2 minutes, then repeat the procedure on the opposite side.

PRESSURE POINTS

P6

AN EXTRA TIP

In a tinted glass bottle with a dropper, mix 15ml (½ fl oz) of **apricot kernel oil**, 50 drops of **roman chamomile essential oil**, 25 drops of **ylang-ylang essential oil**, 25 drops of true **lavender essential oil**, 25 drops of **lemon verbena essential oil**, 20 drops of **marjoram essential oil** and 12 drops of **inula essential oil**. Massage 4 to 6 drops on the solar plexus several times a day, as required.

IN TRADITIONAL CHINESE MEDICINE

Palpitations can be attributed to many causes: a long-term illness, excessive thinking or a substantial loss of blood ... These signs cause damage to the heart and the spleen, and lead to a depletion of qi and blood, which are no longer able to ensure the heart's supply. Shen is disturbed, and this creates palpitations. An excess of emotional fire can also be a cause: this leads to a depletion of the kidney's yin and the rupture of balance between the kidney's water and the heart's fire, which disturbs Shen. Long-lasting palpitations or heart disease obstructs the heart's blood vessels, leading to stagnation of qi and blood. The internal accumulation of phlegm, due to a depletion of the heart's yang or a depletion of the spleen and the kidney, also disturbs the heart and Shen and causes palpitations.

Loss of consciousness (resuscitation)

Total duration of treatment:
VARIABLE

A loss of consciousness can occur in a variety of situations: a fall in blood pressure, stroke, sunstroke, convulsions, epilepsy, coma, hysteria/panic attacks, emotional shock ... The person experiences a sudden blackout; their face will go pale, and limbs cold. Strong emotions, a fright and a weak constitution, accentuated by fatigue and standing for a prolonged period of time, can bring on the attack.

PRESSURE POINTS

GV26

METHOD

- Apply very strong pressure to point **GV26** with your index finger. Maintain this for 2 minutes. You could also use the tip of a pencil for a more powerful effect. Do this until the person regains consciousness, while waiting for the emergency services.
- You can also heat point **CV6** with a moxa stick, while waiting for help to arrive. This restores yang-qi and yang-Shen, and, consequently, consciousness.

IN TRADITIONAL CHINESE MEDICINE

Loss of consciousness can occur on two different grounds: depletion and abundance. Depletion is attributed to excessive fatigue or emotional excess (sadness, a scare) with a disturbance in Shen inducing a collapse of qi. Pure yang can no longer be released, which leads to loss of consciousness. A haemorrhage leads to the loss of qi and, where the fluid goes, the qi goes. As blood supports the mental faculties and the seat of Shen, this is followed by a loss of consciousness. In the case of abundance, anger obstructs the chest; the path of qi attacks the head and brings on a loss of consciousness. Excess yang leads to a rise of qi and blood; the sense orifices are obstructed, explaining the loss of consciousness.

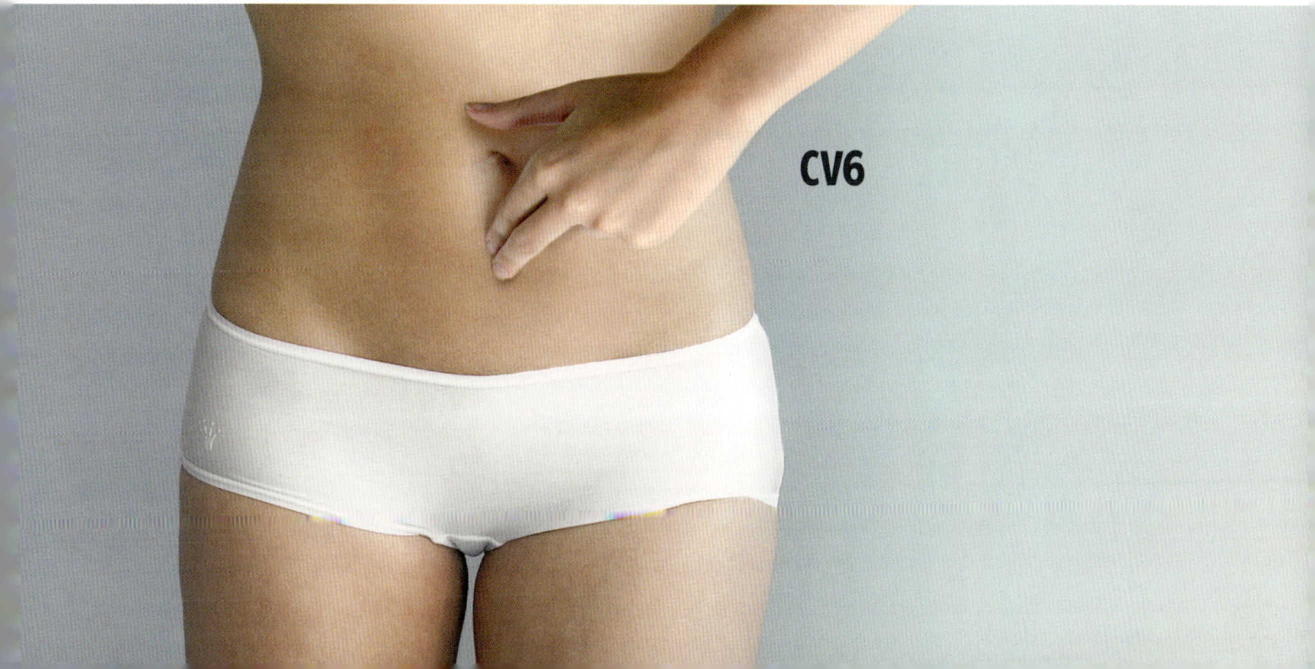

Fears & phobias

Total duration of treatment:
8 MINUTES

Fears are irrepressible, anxiety-inducing dreads and worries that can lead to a state of panic, while phobias are specifically triggered by situations, objects, places or animals which, in themselves, do not present any type of danger. In the absence of the triggering elements, the phobia doesn't manifest, which generates in the subject behaviours of avoidance or reassurance, countering the phobia and allowing the person to cope.

METHOD

Apply moderate pressure to each point with your thumb. Maintain this for 2 minutes, then repeat the procedure on the opposite side.

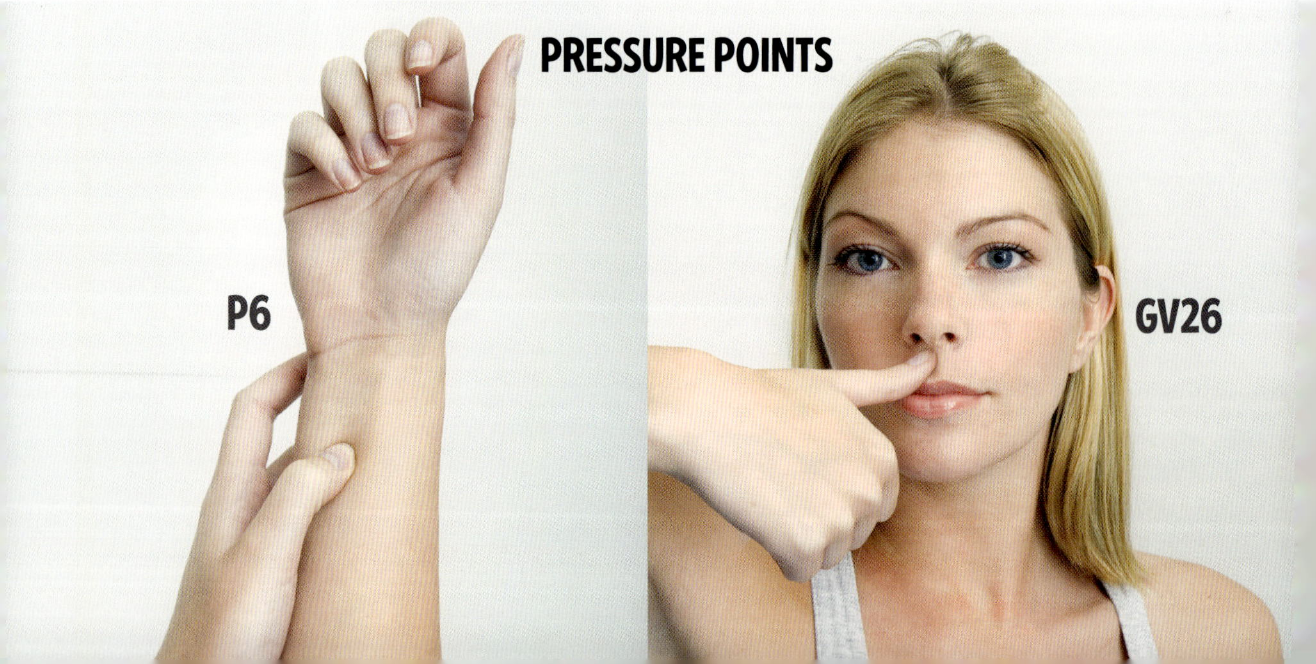

IN AN EMERGENCY

In an absolute emergency, apply strong pressure to point **GV26** with your thumb. Maintain this for 2 minutes. You could also use the tip of a pencil for greater effectiveness. The pain from these stimuli could bring on tears – a good sign.

AN EXTRA TIP

In a tinted glass bottle with a dropper, mix 7.5ml (¼ fl oz) of **apricot kernel oil**, 50 drops of **angelica root essential oil**, 50 drops **cedarwood atlas essential oil** and 12 drops of **katrafay essential oil**. Massage 5 to 10 drops of this preparation onto the solar plexus or the soles of the feet. You could also apply a few drops on your wrists and breathe this in deeply, five times in a row. **Caution**: this preparation is contraindicated for women who are pregnant or breastfeeding, as well as for children under 6 years. Also exercise caution with those suffering from epilepsy. Do not expose yourself to sunlight within 6 to 8 hours of application.

IN TRADITIONAL CHINESE MEDICINE

This category includes fear, chronic anxiety and sudden fright. Fear weakens the kidney's qi, which controls the lower orifices, making qi descend. Examples include bed-wetting in children and urinary incontinence or diarrhoea in adults following a violent scare. A state of anxiety and chronic fear weakens qi, depending on the condition of the heart organ. If it's strong, fear causes qi to descend; if the heart is weak, qi rises and induces signs such as palpitations, insomnia, a dry mouth and throat, and dizziness. The heart-kidney (fire-water) communication route is essential for emotional stability. The heart's qi descends towards the kidney and the kidney's qi ascends towards the heart. If this communication is cut off, chronic anxiety makes the rise of the kidney's qi impossible and impedes it. The heart's qi cannot descend towards the kidney, and thus the kidney cannot ground it. Fear and phobias then set in.

Anxiety & stress

Total duration of treatment:
12 MINUTES

Anxiety is a normal reaction to stress, a phenomenon which allows the body to deal with events. But when this transforms into psychological distress relating to the irrational fear of a real or imaginary threat, it can turn into a disabling disorder. Certain subjective and objective physical phenomena are characteristic of this type of anxiety, including: motor tension, trembling, fatigue, dry mouth, sweating, tachycardia, chest or abdominal tightness, panic attacks, obsessive-compulsive disorders, post-traumatic stress disorders, social or social anxiety disorders and specific phobia. Anti-anxiety treatments are standard. For generalized anxiety associated with a depressive tendency, treatment with antidepressants is usually recommended.

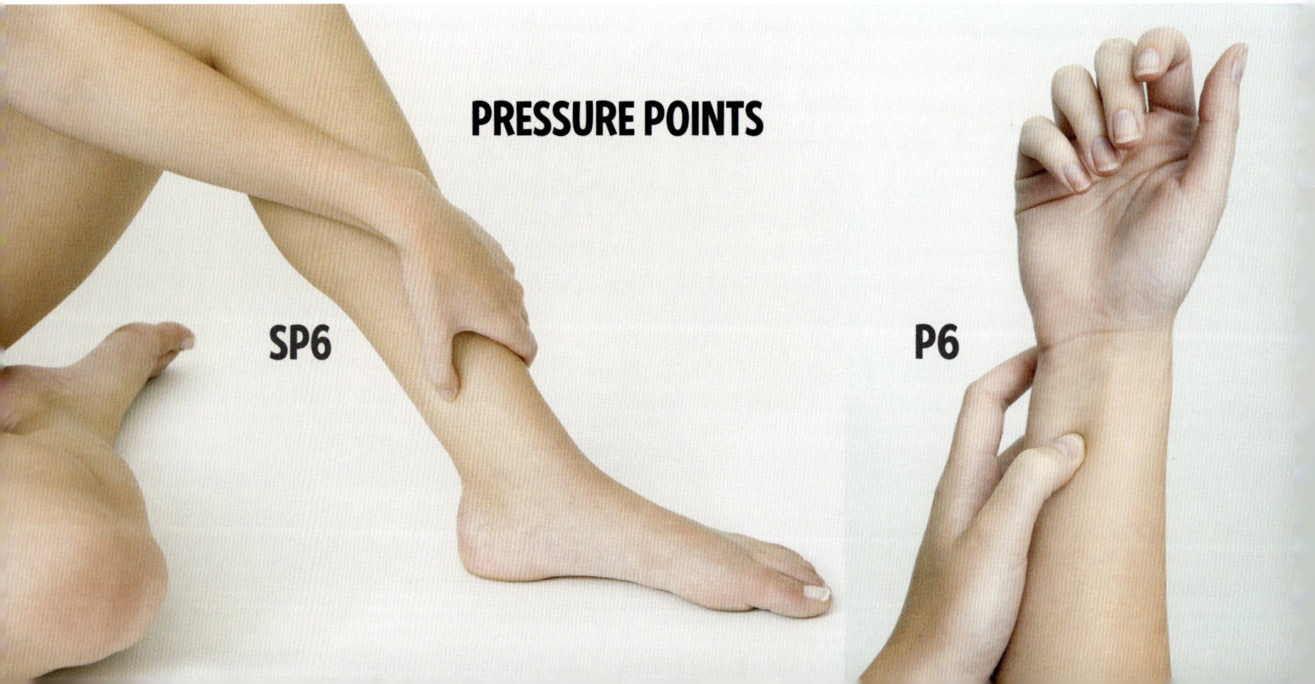

METHOD

Apply moderate pressure on each point with your thumb until you sense pain. Maintain for 2 minutes, then repeat the procedure on the opposite side.

IN AN EMERGENCY

In cases of acute stress, strongly stimulate pressure point **GV26** with your thumbnail or with the tip of a pencil, to restore awareness and calm Shen.

AN EXTRA TIP

The mineral **magnesium** is an excellent anti-stress substance. Opt for cocoa powder or Brazil nuts. You may also want to consider taking a supplement: consult your doctor for advice.

IN TRADITIONAL CHINESE MEDICINE

In Chinese medical literature there is no term that specifically describes what we would call 'anxiety' or 'stress' in the West. Traditional clinical cases reflect 'fear and palpitations' (Jing Ji), 'panic-induced heart palpitations' (Zheng Chong) and 'agitation' (Zang Zao). Severe emotions cause stagnation of the liver's qi, generating heat, causing damage to the blood and the yin and producing a blood and/or yin deficiency.

Sleep disorders

Total duration of treatment:
12 MINUTES

Sleep is an essential time for the body to repair and recharge itself, yet a great many people admit to sleeping badly. There are three types of sleeping disorder: insomnia (insufficient sleep), hypersomnia (excessive sleep), and parasomnia (abnormal behaviours during sleep). Many parameters can be involved in these disorders – in particular, certain diseases, overconsumption of stimulants, as well as stress and anxiety ...

METHOD

Apply moderate pressure to each point with your thumb. Maintain this for 2 minutes, then repeat the procedure on the opposite side.

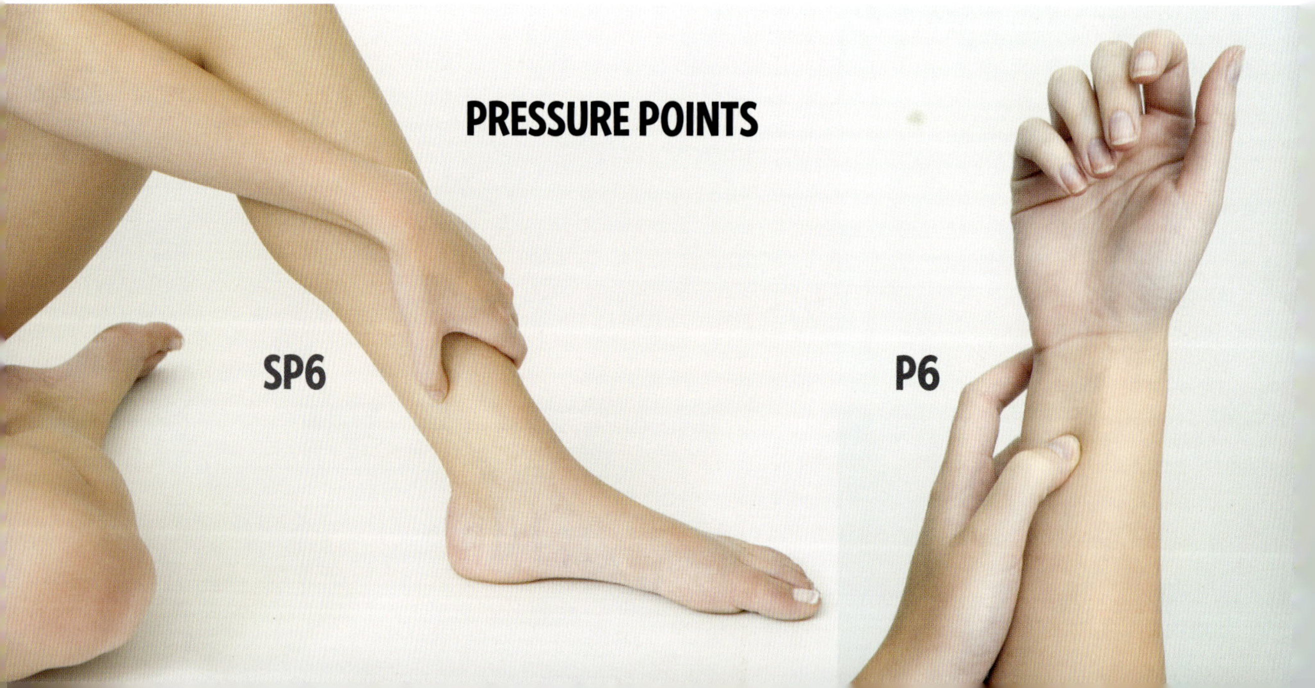

SOME EXTRA TIPS

- In a bottle, mix 15ml (½ fl oz) of **apricot kernel oil**, 7 drops of **neroli essential oil**, 25 drops of **roman chamomile essential oil** and 75 drops of **petitgrain bigarade (bitter orange) essential oil**. Apply 3 to 5 drops of this mixture to the soles of the feet, the solar plexus and the insides of your wrists, and inhale strongly before bed.
- Try **melatonin** supplements.

IN TRADITIONAL CHINESE MEDICINE

Anxiety, excessive thinking and mental rumination cause damage to the heart and the spleen. Shen is no longer stable due to the disorder of the heart's yin-blood, which is its anchoring support. The depletion of the spleen slows down the formation of qi and blood, and the heart becomes undernourished. Mental depression arises through the blockage of the liver's qi, which transforms into fire, rises to disturb Shen and causes sleeping problems. An unhealthy diet could also disturb the spleen-stomach, creating phlegm, which transforms into heat. This blocks the rising and descending movements, and leads to disharmony in digestive function and sleeping disorders. Congenital insufficiency, excessive sexual activity or even an overall weakness can also cause damage to the kidney's yin. The kidney's water no longer rises to inhibit the heart's fire, and disharmony between the kidney's water and the heart's fire brings on these disorders.

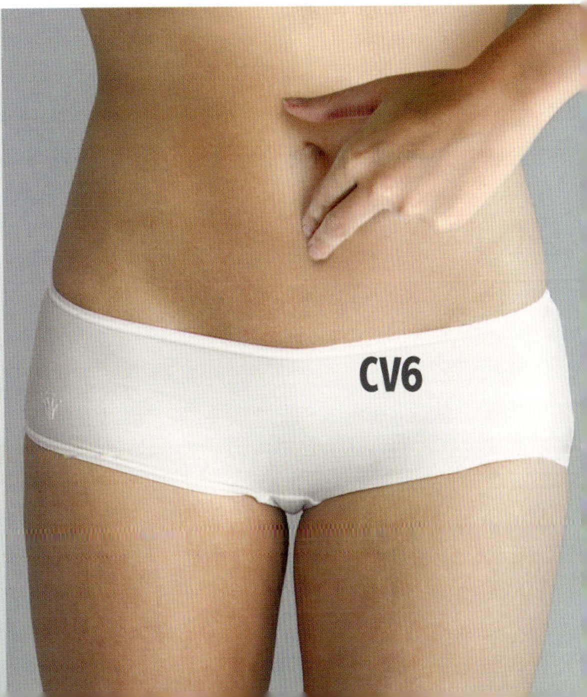

Dizziness

Total duration of treatment:
10 MINUTES

Dizziness is the false sensation of the body's movement or the movement of surrounding objects. In benign cases, it stops when you close your eyes. In more serious cases, it can lead to a fall, and can also be accompanied by nausea, vomiting, perspiration and loss of consciousness.

PRESSURE POINTS

SP6

METHOD

Apply moderate pressure to each point with your thumb. Maintain this for 2 minutes, then repeat the procedure on the opposite side.

AN EXTRA TIP

You could also try traditional energy practices, such as acupuncture and foot reflexology.

VARIATION

Try heating point **GV20** with a moxa stick for 5 minutes, as long as there are no signs of heat (fever, heat and redness of the skin) or arterial hypertension.

IN TRADITIONAL CHINESE MEDICINE

Dizziness can be caused by an excessive rise of the liver's yang, an insufficiency of the kidney's essence, a deficit of qi and blood, an internal accumulation of humidity, and an obstruction of the meridians by stagnant or coagulated blood.

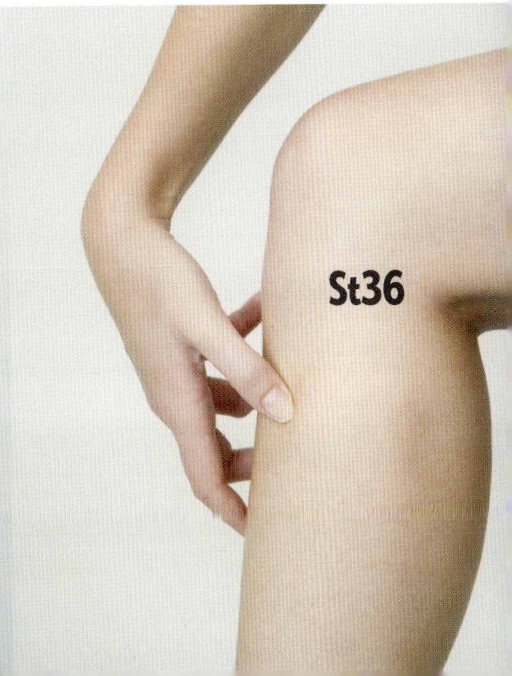

Strengthening immunity

Total duration of treatment:
10 MINUTES

The immune system's function is to prevent germs from penetrating, and to inhibit attacks when the primary barriers of the body's defences are attacked. The immune system prevents infections (from bacteria, viruses, and the like). It guarantees our internal equilibrium, helping to distinguish between the 'self' and the 'non-self', to neutralize and destroy intruders. An imbalance in this function leads to autoimmune diseases. The effectiveness of the immune system resides in its immuno-surveillance role.

METHOD

- Heat the points with a moxa stick until the area becomes red. Generally, about 10 minutes is sufficient.
- Alternatively, you could also use acupressure by applying moderate pressure to these points with your thumb, until you sense pain. Maintain this for 3 minutes, then repeat on the opposite side.

MOXIBUSTION & IMMUNITY

Moxibustion is an ancient technique for longevity. It improves the immune functions by helping the body eliminate pathogens, strengthening the body and extending life. Used as a preventative measure, it helps reinforce Zheng Qi (true energy) and the body, prevents disease and relapses, and helps prepare for seasonal changes. By regularly practising this self-treatment, you will be working on maintaining your body by strengthening it and thus increasing your longevity.

AN EXTRA TIP

You can complement this by opting for traditional energy practices such as Qi Gong, Tai Chi Chuan, yoga, relaxation, meditation, sophrology (a healthcare philosophy based on the study of consciousness in harmony) and cardiac coherence.

IN TRADITIONAL CHINESE MEDICINE

Immunity can be compared to what we call the true energy or proper energy (Zheng Qi). Consider your body as a kingdom. Throughout the kingdom there are frontiers, and in order to guard these frontiers there is an army. Your army is your Zheng Qi. Depending on the abundance or deficiency of Zheng Qi, you will remain the sovereign of your kingdom (health) or submit to invaders (diseases). An abundance of Zheng Qi guarantees maximum protection for the body against these diseases: the aggressors (viruses, wind-cold-heat-humidity-drought, bacteria, and so on) cannot invade the body. Maintaining the vitality of the body's functions, the yin/yang balance, the organs-bowels and Shen helps reinforce the defence capacity of Zheng Qi.

PRESSURE POINTS

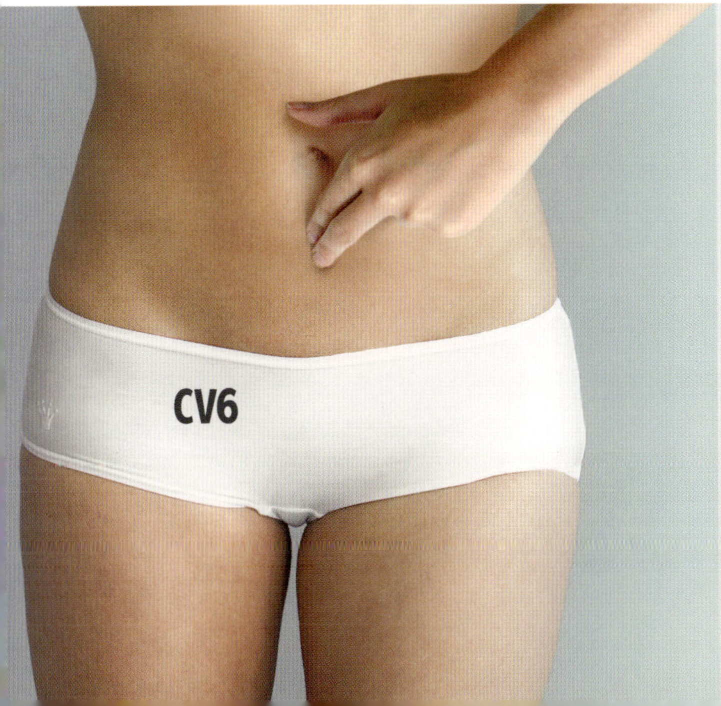

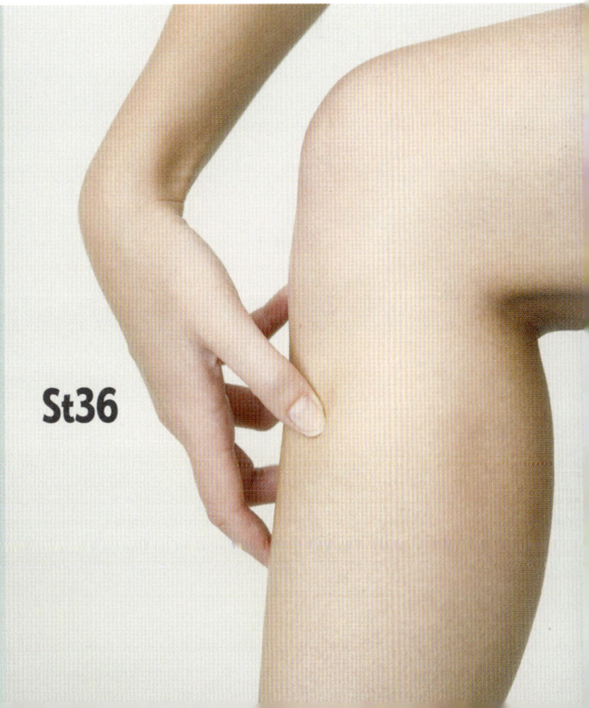

INDEX

A

abdominal pain 96–97
acupressure
  basic principle of 7
  cautions 22–23
  contraindications 23
  holistic solution 7
  meridians 13, 18, 19
  preparation for 24–25
  techniques 24
  uses and benefits 21
allergies, seasonal 80–81, 83
aloe vera 73
angelica root 149
anosmia 88–89
antibiotics, natural 87
anxiety 7, 150–151
apricot kernel 131, 133, 145, 149, 153
aspartame 97
asthma 82–83

B

babies and children 22
back pain 22, 106–107
bad breath 66
Bai Hui 62–63
balsam fir 93
bay laurel 101, 113, 117, 119, 120, 123
bed-wetting 130–131, 149
bergamot mint 133
black spruce 31, 141
bladder 13, 18, 29
bloating and gas 66–67
blond psyllium 67, 69
brain 15, 143
Branching Ditch 56–57
breast pain 104–105
breathing and breathing practice 25
Broken Sequence 54–55

C

calophyllum 107
cardamom 117
cedarwood 149
chamomile herbal tea 67
chamomile oil 101
childbirth 128–129
clary sage 31, 127
clove 125
colds and flu 55, 92–93
colloidal silver 87
consciousness, loss of 146–147
constipation 68–69
copalba 99
copalba balsam 99, 111, 125
coriander 97
cun system 19, 20
cypress 30, 113, 131

D

dairy products, elimination of 73, 81, 84, 91, 95, 97, 114
damask rose 143
depression 7, 98, 99
diarrhoea 66, 70–71
disease, causes of 13–14
dispersion 24
dizziness 14, 149, 154–155
doctor, consulting a 22

E

earth energy 12, 13
echinacea 93
energy *see* qi
energy channels *see* meridians
energy phases 12–13
energy points 18
  see also Pressure Point index entries
epilepsy 61, 138–139, 149
erectile dysfunction 132–133
essential oils 28–31
  cautions 31
  correspondences 29
  diffusion 29
  external use 28
  internal use (ingesting) 28
  oxidation 29
  properties 30–31
eucalyptus globulus 29
eucalyptus radiata 30, 91
extraordinary vessels 19

F

fatigue 140–141
fears and phobias 148–149
fire energy 12, 13
fish oils 81
five movements theory 12–13
flexibility 21

G

gall bladder 13, 18, 29, 77, 99
gastro-oesophageal reflux 75
geranium 29
ginger oil 30, 71, 79
ginger root 79
ginkgo biloba 84
gluten elimination 73, 81, 84, 93, 97, 114, 143

H

hand pain 102–103
harmonization 24
hazelnut 97
He Gu 50–51
headache 22, 120–121, 134
heart 13, 15, 18, 25, 145, 149, 153
helichrysum 101, 107, 117, 123
hiccups 74–75
Huan Tiao 46–47
Hundred Meetings 62–63
hypericum 101, 113, 117, 120, 123

I

imbalances 7, 13, 14
immune system 81
  strengthening 21, 33, 156–157
Inner Gate 52–53
insomnia 7, 152
inula 145

J

Jing (Jing-qi) 14, 15
Joining Valley 50–51
Jumping Circle 46–47
juniper 29, 111

K

katrafay 111, 149
kidneys 13, 15, 18, 85, 87, 91, 101, 109, 119, 127, 131, 137, 143, 145, 149, 153
knee pain 108–109

L

L-Arginine 133
large intestine 13, 18, 85, 119
lavandin 113
lavender 77, 83, 91, 95, 145
leg pain 100–101, 112–113
Leg Three Miles 42–43
lemon eucalyptus 99, 117, 125
lemon verbena 145
lemongrass 111, 141
Lie Que 54–55
life force *see* qi
liver 13, 18, 67, 73, 77, 99, 105, 107, 109, 127, 133, 135, 137, 151
longevity 7, 15, 21, 48, 53, 156
loss of smell 88–89
lumbago 116–117, 122
lumbar pain 112–113
lungs 13, 18, 29, 54, 81, 83, 87, 89, 91, 95, 141
lymphatic system 18

M

macadamia 99, 113, 127
magnesium 151
magnet therapy 77
Man's Middle 60–61
marjoram 31, 89, 145
massage sticks 24
meditation 25
melatonin 153
memory problems 142–143
menopause 35
menstruation 33, 126–127, 134–135

meridians 13, 18, 19
metal energy 12, 13
migraine 120–121
monosodium glutamate 97
motion sickness 76–77
moxa sticks 32, 34, 35
moxibustion 22, 32–35, 156
  cautions 35, 104
  effects of 32
  technique 34–35
  uses and benefits 33
mugwort 32

N
nasal discharge 94, 95
nausea 78–79
Nei Guan 52–53
neroli 153
neuralgia 98, 101
niaouli 29, 31, 83, 93, 95

O
older people 22
omega-3 oils 81
oregano 29
organs and bowels, relationship between 13, 18

P
pain
  back pain 106–107
  breast pain 104–105
  causes of 21, 32, 107, 109, 111, 113, 115, 123
  generalized aches and pains 114–115
  hand pain 102–103
  knee pain 108–109
  leg pain 100–101, 112–113
  lumbago 116–117
  lumbar pain 112–113
  painful periods 134–135
  relief of 22, 51
  rib pain 98–99
  sciatica 122–123
  toothache 118–119
  wrist pain 110–111
palpitations 144–145, 149
peace and serenity 21
pear tea 87
peppermint 29, 31, 67, 77, 86, 93, 101, 113, 123
periods
  absence of 126–127
  painful 134–135
petitgrain bigarade (bitter orange) 153
pistacia lentiscus/mastic pistachio 107
prebiotics 69
pregnant women 22, 31, 35, 40, 49, 51, 149
Pressure Point CV6 22, 38, 39, 48–49
Pressure Point GB30 38, 39, 46–47
Pressure Point GV20 38, 39, 62–63
Pressure Point GV26 38, 39, 60–61
Pressure Point LI4 22, 38, 39, 50–51
Pressure Point LI20 38, 39, 58–59
Pressure Point Lu7 38, 39, 54–55
Pressure Point P6 38, 39, 52–53
Pressure Point Sp6 22, 38, 39, 40–41
Pressure Point St36 33, 38, 39, 42–43
Pressure Point TB6 38, 39, 56–57
Pressure Point UB40 38, 39, 44–45
probiotics 73, 81
propolis 91
prostate 29

Q
qi 10, 13, 14, 15, 18, 21, 33
  blockage of 21, 22, 73
  parental qi 15
Qi Hai 48–49

R
ravintsara 93, 141
Ren Zhong 60–61
rhinitis 90–91
ribs, pain in the 98–99
roman chamomile 97, 123, 135, 145, 153
rosemary 29, 30, 89, 91, 113, 125

S
sage 127, 135, 141
St John's Wort *see* hypericum
San Yin Jiao 40–41
sandalwood 29
sciatica 22, 101, 122–123
Sea of Qi 48–49
Shen 14, 15, 138, 145, 147
Siam wood 133
sinusitis 94–95
sleep disorders 152–153
small intestine 13, 18
sore throat 86–87
spikenard 31, 89
spleen 13, 18, 29, 67, 73, 83, 91, 109, 141, 153
stiff neck 124–125
stomach 13, 18, 79, 85, 109, 119, 141
stomach pains 72–73
stress 7, 13, 99, 101, 123, 150–151
Supporting Middle 44–45
sweet almond 83, 91, 95
sweet fennel 97

T
tarragon 75, 97, 135
tea tree 30, 141
Three Treasures 14–15
Three Yin Intersection 40–41
thuja 31
thyme 93, 101, 123
thyme thujanol 141
tinnitus 84–85
tonification 24
toothache 118–119
torticolis 124–125
Traditional Chinese Medicine
  disease, theory of 13–14
  five movements theory 12–13
  key concepts 10–11
  pain, theory of 21, 32
  Three Treasures 14–15
tropical basil 120

U
urinary incontinence 130–131, 149
urinary problems 136–137

V
visualization 24
vomiting 78–79

W
water energy 12, 13
Wei Zhong 44–45
Welcome Fragrance 58–59
wild mint 120
wind 13–14, 83, 93, 95
wintergreen 99, 101, 113, 120, 123, 125
wood energy 12, 13
wrist pain 110–111

Y
yin and yang 10–11, 12, 13, 14, 15, 18
  correspondences 10
  symbol 11
Ying Xiang 58–59
ylang-ylang 101, 120, 123, 135, 145

Z
Zheng Qi 156, 157
Zhi Gou 56–57
Zu San Li 42–43

ABOUT THE AUTHORS

Laurent Turlin is a Traditional Chinese Medicine practitioner and qualified acupuncturist, teaching and practising acupuncture at his clinic in Paris. Having studied for five years in Europe and two years in China, he then developed his method of treatment based on energy anatomy from the teachings of Tibetan Master Djwhal Khul. He also trained with, and was an assistant to, Philippe Sionneau, a renowned expert on the subject of Chinese medicine.

Written in collaboration with **Alix Lefief-Delcourt**, a journalist specializing in natural health topics, food, organic living and cookery.

PICTURE CREDITS

Cover Image Point Fr/ShutterStockphoto.Inc

ShutterStockphoto.Inc 2-3 Image Point Fr; 6-7 Tom Wang; 8-9 Image Point Fr; 16-17 Image Point Fr; 19bl Zemler; 19cl Studio concept; 19cr & br Alexey Boldin; 20 Sue Atkinson; 23 Image Point Fr; 25 Luna Vandoorne; 26-27 Image Point Fr; 29 Image Point Fr; 30 Melpomene; 32 Africa Studio; 36-7 sirtravelalot; 39 Sue Atkinson.

All photos on pages 40 to 157 Image Point Fr/ShutterStockphoto.Inc

ACKNOWLEDGEMENTS

Eddison Books Limited
Creative Consultant **Nick Eddison**
Managing Editor **Tessa Monina**
Design **Jane McKenna** (www.fogdog.co.uk)
Translator **Lalit Nadkarni**
Proofreader **Nikky Twyman**
Indexer **Marie Lorimer**
Production **Sarah Rooney**

With thanks to Leduc.s Éditions, Paris